READYMADE INTERVIEW QUESTIONS

3rd edition

malcolm peel
revised by margaret dale

KOGAN PAGE

First published in 1988
Second edition 1996
Third edition 2001

Kogan Page Limited
120 Pentonville Road
London N1 9JN

British Library Cataloguing in Publication Data

A CIP record for this book is available from the British Library.

ISBN 0 7494 3621 2

Typeset by JS Typesetting, Wellingborough, Northants
Printed and bound in Great Britain by Clays Ltd, St Ives plc

Contents

Contents _____

Introduction

The importance of selecting the right candidate

The point of having a selection process is to enable you to predict which of all the candidates who have expressed an interest in the job vacancy will be the right person. Making a selection decision is possibly the most important one you are able to make on behalf of your employer, so making sure that the right person is appointed is important to you.

But this is also a decision with risks and costs, with the risks being perhaps more important than the costs. Offering someone a job creates a legally binding contract with rights and responsibilities on both sides. Yet some techniques used in selection have as much predictive power as simply pulling someone in from the street. While this method is seldom used, others that are not much better, like the unstructured interview, are often employed.

A good interview that is likely to result in the right candidate being offered the job is designed, carefully planned and staged. The questions asked are also planned and put to the candidates in a way that gives them all reasonable opportunity to present themselves in their best light.

Deciding who to appoint

Most people believe themselves to be good judges of others. But those with experience of conducting any form of structured assessment are aware of the complexity of human character and relationships. They will have learnt something of the problems of trying to predict behaviour, especially in a new environment, and know that there can be no short cuts and no certainty in choosing people.

The steps needed to reduce the risk of making a mistake and improve the quality of prediction are not hard or complicated, as will be discussed. However, this book is not intended to discuss the whole process at length; there are other books noted in the bibliography that do this better.

The cost of selection

Choosing someone for a post is a major capital investment. The costs include:

- advertising;
- agency or consultant fees (if used);
- management and administrative time, including;
  - documentation;
  - shortlisting;
  - interviewing;
  - hidden overhead costs;
- candidates' expenses;
- relocation (if paid);
- salary and employment costs.

For a senior post, these are likely to total many thousands of pounds.

The opportunity cost of failing to appoint the right person can be far higher than those associated with the risks above. Not only will you lose the pay-off from their skills, but a competitor will be sure to gain. In a top level job, the cost of losing opportunities for expansion and growth that your competitors gain may be almost infinite. If you make this error, in a worst-case scenario, the entire future of your organization could be destroyed at a stroke.

The problems of rectification

'Appoint in haste, repent at leisure' is a motto worth a place on the wall of every interviewer. Putting things right after a mistaken selection decision may be traumatic and costly.

Discovering the mistake will involve assessing performance accurately and quickly. Facing the discovery will call for moral courage and interpersonal skill. Dismissing the person will present procedural difficulties and possibly legal aspects. Even at its easiest, the termination process will be highly unpleasant.

There will also be direct costs. You will lose from the mistakes and poor performance during the period of employment. There may be physical damage, waste, lost business, upset customers or demotivated colleagues. Compensation might be payable, and perhaps wages in lieu of notice. At the end of it all, you will have to face a second round of expense in trying to make a better choice.

Perhaps the worst case is the employee who is not quite bad enough to dismiss, but whose performance is not up to standard. Such a person may not fit into the team yet there are insufficient grounds to terminate him or her, so the individual remains in the organisation as a memory of an interviewer's poor decision.

The two-way fit

Selection involves matching people and jobs. But there are two sides to every match: the satisfaction of the employer and that of the candidate. Both must decide how close the match is likely to be and whether they are likely to achieve their desired outcomes. Both must try to foresee the future. Both are entitled to their opinion. Either or both may make a mistake, and whichever it is, the damage will be equally serious.

Employers have the power to make or withhold an offer of employment, they may be tempted to overplay their hand. If the market conditions allow, they may pressurize candidates into accepting unfair offers. They may make false claims about what the job offers, or fail to point out its drawbacks or difficulties.

Candidates may make unjustified claims about the level or extent of their experience. They may go beyond the bounds of honesty, claiming false qualifications or hiding material facts. They may play employers off against one another.

When any of these things happen, both parties stand to suffer. Selection cannot be one way; the employer is choosing an employee, and the candidate is choosing an employer. Both are making a serious and difficult decision. Both will need to use all their skill and every aid available to have the best chance of success.

The plan of this book

The principal aim of this book is to supply a number of interview questions. To use these questions effectively, you must put them into context. They do not purport to hold the keys to success, for good questions are of no value by themselves; used wrongly, they may even do harm. They must be asked correctly and sensitively at the right time, as part of a systematic and thorough process.

The book is therefore organized in two parts. Part 1 looks at the recruitment process, and Part 2 suggests readymade questions.

1. The selection process

This is summarized briefly in Chapter 1. Those readers who are already familiar with the process will wish to pass over this ground quickly. Those who wish to know more are referred to books and sources listed in the Bibliography.

2. Selection interviewing

The interview is, of course, only one part of the selection process. The interview is described in some detail in Chapter 2. Those who are familiar with interviewing may wish at least to glance through what is said to see how closely their own ideas match the approach suggested there. Those who wish to study the subject in greater depth may wish to select additional reading from the Bibliography.

3. Questioning

The interview is the place where the employer and candidate meet to exchange information. This is done through a series of questions and answers. Chapter 3 contains a description of the art of asking questions. To get the best value from the questions offered in Part 2, you are recommended to devote time to this chapter.

The questions

Part 2, Chapters 4 to 10, contains suggested questions for you to consider and adapt to your own interviewing purposes.

As asking questions is of no value by itself, each question is followed by a selection of typical answers, to each of which a possible interpretation is given.

It is not suggested that all the questions are used for each candidate; this would be ineffective and impracticable. The hope is that you will select from the questions offered those that meet your needs best. Some will be selected in advance as part of the preparation for each interview. The others may be used as supplementary probes to gather extra information or to check data submitted elsewhere. You should ensure that all candidates are treated consistently and that they are asked questions about the same topic areas. This does not mean you have to slavishly follow a rigid script. However, you should not give a candidate grounds for accusations of unfair or discriminatory treatment simply because you asked him or her a question not put to the other candidates.

You will not find trick questions designed simply to catch the candidate out or load him or her with embarrassment. Such questions rarely help, and may well hinder good selection. The candidate usually senses that a game is being played and as a result may decide to seek employment elsewhere. Thus, you might lose the best candidate and damage your reputation. Well-conducted interviews, on the other hand, go a long way to enhancing your reputation as well as forming the basis of a productive and happy working relationship.

Getting the interview right is not rocket science, nor does it require lots of money and time. It simply requires thought, planning and placing yourself in the candidates' shoes. If you treat them in the way that you would expect to be treated by a good employer, you will not go far wrong.

Part 1

The recruitment process

The recruitment process

To be effective, the recruitment process must follow a number of steps. These are:

1. defining the job;
2. establishing the person specification;
3. designing the recruitment and selection process;
4. making the vacancy known;
5. deciding how applications are to be made;
6. receiving and documenting applications;
7. running the selection process;
8. carrying out final checks;
9. offering employment and agreeing terms and conditions of contract;
10. induction.

Defining the job

Unless you know *why* you need to recruit someone, there can be little hope of appointing the right person. Everyone involved must know, and agree with everyone else, what job is to be done.

Is the job necessary at all?

The first question to be asked will always be 'Is there really a post to be filled?' When a vacancy occurs, one thinks automatically of filling it, but this is an ideal opportunity to examine the situation, consider whether and how to restructure how the work is done and who does it. The need to recruit can also arise from the growth of a new area of work. Unless the job is carefully designed, it can be very easy to appoint the wrong kind of person. It may be that no one is needed, or that a very different type of job with different demands needs to be filled.

The job description

Most larger organizations have written job descriptions for each post.

Smaller organizations may not have written descriptions. But even in the smallest organisation, the discipline of writing a description helps to clarify thinking, and to explain the job to everyone else involved.

At the least, the description will need to cover:

- job title;
- the purpose of the post;
- who it reports to;
- the duties and key objectives.

Depending on your needs, you may also include:

- department;
- grade or salary range;
- responsibility for other staff;
- relationships with other departments/posts;
- external relationships.

An example is shown opposite.

The vacancy provides the opportunity to take out, review and update the job description. The manager responsible for the post, the personnel professionals and the outgoing occupant may be able to contribute to this review. There are several pitfalls to look out for.

The description may not be up to date. The job will need to be structured and described for the *next* occupant, not for the last.

The description may give little guidance as to what is actually to be done. For effective recruitment and performance of the job the description may need to be rewritten or supplemented with additional information.

Job description

<u>Job title</u>	Manager, Learning Resources Centre
<u>Reporting to</u>	Director of Personnel
<u>Staff responsibilities</u>	2 Information Researchers; 1 Training Adviser; 2 Customer Service Assistants
<u>Duties</u>	To meet the information and development training needs of the Institute's members and staff
	To manage the resources and personnel of the Centre so its mission is achieved efficiently and effectively
	To use current and developing technology effectively for the delivery of the services and operation of the centre
	To agree the Centre's financial budget and business plan and work within them
	To market the services provided by the Centre
<u>Relationships (internal)</u>	All Institute Heads of Department, training providers, council and other members
<u>Relationships (external)</u>	Those responsible for providing similar services in other organizations and related professional bodies.

The description may be too rigid and restricting. The way many jobs are performed may legitimately reflect the skills and interests of the job holder. This may be the case, for example, with creative, academic or professional posts, or when an area of work is split between a number of similar posts. In such situations, job descript-ions need to be flexible, but this should not be an excuse for woolly thinking. A good job description clearly sets out the work to be done, using active verbs. The use of objectives – what is to be achieved – also helps to explain the job and supports the future review of performance.

Now and then, writing a job description may cause a fund-amental change in thinking; perhaps the post could be abolished; three separate posts may be required; perhaps the whole area of work should be restructured; perhaps the desired outcomes are impossible to meet.

The person specification

Having defined the job, we must describe the sort of person who would best fill it.

Generating possible factors

Great care needs to be taken when drawing up this document to avoid building in stereotypical or outdated factors. As it can be very easy to include elements that may be discriminatory, it is recommended that a structure be used to focus thinking on to the actual needs of the job. This will help the people involved in creating the person specification to think about what the newly appointed person will need to do in the *future* rather than what the previous job holder did.

A useful structure will contain components that describe the future jobholder's:

■ *attainments* – educational and training achievements; certificates gained and milestones passed;
■ *achievements* – track record, work and personal successes;
■ *abilities* – skills and competencies;
■ *aptitudes* – what the person needs to be good at, including factors such as communication and interpersonal skills, problem solving and working on their own initiative, preference for working alone and/or with others.

People other than the manager can be involved in creating the specification. This is best done in a brainstorming session. After suggestions have been gathered, their comparative contribution to the successful performance of the job can be tested and the document revised to:

- cut out unsuitable factors;
- add factors that have been overlooked;
- eliminate duplication and overlapping factors;
- clarify and tighten the wording.

Identifying selection criteria

Decision making is made easier if candidates can be assessed against explicit criteria. If a candidate fails to satisfy one of the essential factors he or she can be eliminated from further consideration. It is particularly useful if some factors can be judged on paper, without the trouble and expense of interviewing – what is sometimes called, 'pre-selection' or 'shortlisting'.

The factors must not be invented for the sake of it or set at impossibly high levels, or perfectly good candidates will be eliminated.

It is essential that factors can be assessed objectively. 'Must be of smart appearance', 'articulate', or 'credible to senior management', for example, cannot be used as they are subjective and cannot be assessed and interpreted consistently by all those involved in the recruitment and selection process.

The factors regarded as important but not essential for satisfactory performance of the job are deemed to be 'desirable'. These can be weighted to make it easier to distinguish between candidates, and are particularly useful if there appear to be a lot of suitable candidates.

Once agreed, the person specification, together with the job description, can be used throughout the recruitment and selection process. These documents will form the basis for any advertisement or other material sent to prospective candidates. The person specification will provide the criteria against which shortlisting decisions will be made. It will also form the basis for the design and choice of selection methods and will help to structure interviews. A person specification for the job of Learning Resource Manager is given on page 14.

Manager, Learning Resource Centre – Person Specification

Essential

- A university degree (2.1 or above).
- Experience of staff management and training delivery.
- The ability to communicate clearly in writing and orally.
- Commitment to supporting and stimulating the learning of others.

Desirable

- A librarianship qualification.
- A qualification or certificated training in teaching or training.
- Experience of working in an institutional or public library, information or resource centre.
- Computer literacy and experience of using information technology and multimedia learning resources.
- Experience of budget management and the preparation of business plans.
- Experience of marketing and promotion.
- Ability to act on initiative and overcome difficulties.
- Commitment to the provision of quality services.

Designing the recruitment and selection process

Once the job description and person specification have been finalized, it is important to design and plan the whole of the recruitment and selection process. This will enable it to be kept on time and on budget, and will increase the chances of appointing the best available candidate.

The process, the component stages of which have already been outlined, can be viewed in the same light as any other project and can benefit from the use of normal project management skills. These

include planning, identification and effective deployment of resources, monitoring progress and taking remedial action if needed.

Providing information

Publicizing the vacancy can be done in one of several ways or by
using a combination. In terms of actual expenditure this can be
the most costly element, but in fact other stages of the process can
consume equal amounts of valuable resources – especially if the
use of management and professional time is not effective. Also, it
is easy to forget that potential candidates' experience of the organization forms their impressions of it as an employer. Badly written
letters and poor-quality information do little to attract a good pool
of candidates.

Ways of applying

After deciding how to publicize the vacancy, consideration needs
to be given to:

1. how the candidates are to apply;
2. what additional information to give them.

Many organizations expect candidates to submit letters of application and/or send in curriculum vitae. Others send out printed
application forms – this provides the opportunity to supply the
applicant with more information than can be contained in an
advertisement. While both the application form and the information
pack need to be designed and prepared, processes with associated
costs, you can save time by ensuring that all candidates receive
and supply the same information in a similar format.

Shortlisting

The processing of the applications on receipt is the point at which
the first of the selection decisions is made. It therefore deserves as
much attention as the final decision. The factors contained in the
person specification can be used to distinguish candidates who are
evidently unsuitable from those who merit further consideration.

Shortlisting can be done in several stages, not all of which require
the involvement of managers. If the person specification contains

clear 'must-have' criteria, such as the possession of certain qualifications or a certain amount of management or direct customer service experience, administrative staff can examine the applications and separate out those that do not meet the essential criteria. This leaves the more detailed consideration to the managers or professional recruiter.

Regardless of who sifts the applications, it is important that the reasons behind a decision to shortlist or reject an application are clear and are recorded. If the decision is queried at any point, these contemporary records are invaluable.

Selection methods

There are several selection methods that can be used separately or combined. The choice of method will depend on the nature of the job in question, the organization's culture and history, and the skills of the staff involved. The interview is the most frequently used method, yet research suggests that it is the poorest way of predicting the performance of a person appointed to a job. Despite its shortcomings, there are good reasons for using an interview – especially as improvements to the method are comparatively easy to make.

While some of the other methods have better predictive powers, misuse and inappropriate use can hinder decision making and reduce the quality of the process in the eyes of the candidate.

Spending time at the outset to decide which method(s) to use and how and when to use them can lead to a highly effective selection process that leaves even the candidates who are not successful with a positive impression. If candidates feel that they have had the opportunity to demonstrate their abilities and have been treated fairly, they will have a good lasting impression of the organization. On the other hand, if candidates feel that they have not been assessed on job-related criteria, that other candidates have been given undue advantage and that decisions have been made on other (non-explicit) grounds, there is a greater chance of them claiming unfair discrimination.

Timescales

Filling a vacant post can take a long time – too long for some managers. However, when the size of the investment and the possible consequences of making a wrong decision are considered, the value of taking the right amount of time is more understandable. For example, it is not unreasonable to allow up to two weeks for candidates to submit their applications. Reading applications and drawing up a shortlist can take a long time and, if managers are involved, the process will need to be fitted in with other duties.

The amount of notice given to candidates regarding the interview will also need to be considered, especially during holiday times, if they have to travel long distances or if the selection process will last a day or more. Candidates may need to ask permission to be away from work, book holiday, arrange cover or alter other plans. Expecting them just to drop things does not necessarily create the best image of their potential future employer.

Making the vacancy known

The aim is to make all *suitable* candidates aware of the vacancy. But if a large number of *unsuitable* candidates apply they will clog up the works and make the task of differentiating between them difficult.

Ideally, the suitable candidates will apply and the unsuitable will select themselves out and not apply.

The vacancy can be made known by:

- word of mouth;
- internal advertisement;
- external advertisement;
- jobcentres;
- private agencies, consultants or headhunters.

Word of mouth

This method must not be neglected, as many vacancies are filled by candidates who have learnt of them from friends, colleagues or neighbours. However, if used alone this method may be regarded as discriminatory as only a limited pool of potential applicants are made aware of the vacancy. Also, the method denies possible good candidates the chance to apply. Therefore, word of mouth must be supplemented by correct, adequate advertising – especially when the appointment or promotion process needs to be transparent and the decision made on the basis of merit. In such cases, justice must both be done and be seen to be done.

Internal advertisement

Many organizations fill vacancies from their existing staff whenever they can, and use procedures to ensure that this policy is followed.

These usually involve the publication of single job advertisements or regular lists of vacancies. Such advertisements will not usually need to be as detailed as external advertisements, as the background and such matters as salary and conditions of employment will generally be well known to possible candidates.

External advertisement

Candidates are frequently sought through advertisements.

Traditionally, factory gate notice-boards were used to display a list of current vacancies, although this medium was usually restricted to unskilled jobs.

These days, jobs are more frequently advertised in newspapers. Less specialized jobs which are likely to be filled by those already living within easy travelling distance may be advertised in local newspapers. Higher level and more specialist posts may be advertised in national newspapers, and senior specialist posts may be advertised in the appropriate professional journals.

National advertising is a costly business, and early decisions will be needed regarding how much to spend. Space is expensive and in a competitive labour market, good design and copy writing can make all the difference. Some employers find it cost effective to use the services of a recruitment agency to design and place the advert.

Writing good recruitment advertisements is not easy. A good advertisement is one that sells the job *and* the organization, and attracts suitable candidates, ie ones that have a reasonable chance of being appointed. It tells potential applicants clearly and concisely what the job entails, what attainments and abilities are essential and what rewards are available to the person appointed. If the advertisement does its job well, it will discourage applications from those who do not meet the essential criteria, thereby saving everyone's time and effort.

A good advertisement contains details of:

- The post's title and its key duties.
- The employer's name (some employers prefer to remain anonymous and use PO Boxes or the services of a recruitment consultancy. Others use their reputation as a means of attracting attention to the vacancy).
- Location (sometimes jobs are not located in any one place and there is an expectation that employees will be prepared to move between sites. However some candidates may be reluctant to change their home base and will want to know where they will be based if successful before they apply for the job).
- Salary and other rewards (there may be times when the employer does not want to give details of the rates of pay, for example, for competitive reasons or because of labour market volatility. However the lack of information may lead to applications from individuals whose expectations are too high. If at all possible, it is better to give an indication of the salary range by using *'circa'*. Details of other rewards can be included to attract applicants who may be seeking benefits such as membership of pension and health schemes, access to training and development opportunities or the potential of career advancement).
- Attainments and abilities that are essential requirements (these can be taken straight from the person specification).
- Other benefits (these can include being in a friendly team, interesting work, access to learning resources).
- How to apply (applicants should be told whether to send for an application form or to submit a letter with or without a CV. Some employers provide additional information in the form of a recruitment pack or have someone available to answer queries).
- The closing date for the receipt of applications.

Most recruitment advertisements in the national or professional press are in display or semi-display format. This generally means that they contain some element of design. The typical situation-vacant text advertisements are called 'lineage ads' and tend to be very brief. Display ads are most costly as they take space. Generally it is better to use the services of a professional agency that can use its buying power to negotiate rates with the publisher, design the advertisement in its entirety and draft the copy. The design of the advertisement is what attracts the jobseeker's eye as it competes with all the others on the page for attention. In a buoyant labour market, the attractiveness of the advertisement, never mind the appeal of the job, can make a considerable difference.

Recruitment advertising is covered by equal opportunities legislation. For the most part, the application of common sense is sufficient to protect an employer from falling into the pitfalls. For example, advertising for a 'Girl Friday' or an 'Odd-job Man' is clearly unacceptable. If you have any doubt, the most advisable course of action is to check. Most newspapers are knowledgeable and competent recruitment consultancies are well aware of legislation.

The Internet is a well-established source of vacancy advertisements and is no longer the preserve of the IT and finance industries. Many recruitment agencies list their stock of vacancies on their Web pages and most main newspapers either have their own site or have their recruitment pages included on a host's site. Fish4jobs.co.uk is an example of such a source which lists jobs taken from most of the regional newspapers.

The professional press and trade press are increasingly making their job pages available on the Internet. Sometimes it is possible to access them directly, but for some it is necessary for jobseekers to register. As with any other source, the employers are expected to pay for the service rather than the jobseeker.

Jobcentres

Jobcentres can offer quick and efficient help with less specialized vacancies. The staff of the Centre will advise on the wording of the advertisement, which will be displayed in the Centre and on the Employment Service's Web site. These are drawn to the attention of suitable jobseekers. There are a number of government schemes aimed at helping disadvantaged jobseekers obtain employment. Some of these offer inducements and support to employers to encourage them to give these people an opportunity. Details are available from jobcentre staff, whose services are free.

Employment agencies, recruitment consultants or search consultants

The *agency* operates by building up a file of people who may be interested in and qualified for certain kinds of vacancy (eg typists, computer operators, accounts clerks etc). It will usually interview people before putting their details on its files.

The agency can then respond to requests by employers for staff by submitting details of those who match their needs, and if required, arranging for them to be considered for selection. An agency may also approach employers, offering to put them in touch with staff on their books who may be suitable for their needs.

Staff engaged to fill a temporary gap are normally paid by the agency, but if offered a permanent post a fee would be paid to the agency, usually on the basis of a percentage of salary. By law, agencies must not charge applicants.

The *recruitment consultant* works primarily by accepting a brief to help fill a specific vacancy for an employer. The consultant will carry out the first stages of the selection process on behalf of the employer; preparing and placing advertisements, receiving applic-ations, shortlisting, carrying out preliminary interviews and possibly others. The employer will complete the selection by conducting final interviews (at which the consultant may or may not be present) and making the choice.

The recruitment consultant also will be paid on the basis of a percentage of salary, together with any costs, such as advertising and printing, that have been incurred.

Use of a consultant enables the employer who does not recruit regularly to save time and effort, and to make use of the skills of the consultant, particularly in specialized areas. It also allows the employer to preserve anonymity until the later stages in the process.

Search consultants are often called *headhunters*. They are given a brief from an employer to help fill a specific vacancy, which is usually at a high level or requires unusual skills or experience. The consultant will then try to find and interest suitable candidates, by direct personal approach or through mutual contacts. The process is usually conducted in the strictest confidence and will not involve advertising.

Deciding how applications are to be made

If a recruitment consultant or employment agency is not to be used, consideration will need to be given as to how to ask candidates to submit their applications. Most often, candidates express their interest in a vacancy on an application form, in a letter of application or by sending in a copy of their curriculum vitae.

The curriculum vitae (CV)

This document is a summary of an individual's work history and usually contains details of educational and other attainments. Tradition dictates that a CV should be brief and, if possible, not more than a page in length. This means that a lot of potentially important information can be missed out. It is also very easy to conceal gaps in employment and make generalized claims about achievement and levels of responsibility that are difficult to check.

The advantages offered by a CV are that the person assessing an application can read it and make quick decisions about whether the applicant satisfies the essential criteria. The applicant can send in a copy of his or her CV very quickly after the advertisement is published and the employer does not have to bear the costs associated with producing and sending out applications forms.

The application form

The application form is important in the selection process. It can be used in the early stages to decide whether to take applications further. For basic posts, its completion can be used as a simple test of literacy, but there is no guarantee of it being filled in by the candidate. It will help you to prepare for and conduct the interview. If the candidate is appointed, it will form part of the personal record. If any important facts (eg qualifications, periods of experience etc) had been seriously misstated, it is possible to terminate the employment or take other disciplinary action.

Design

Standard application forms are widely available, either commercially or in reference books. If there is a need to design one afresh, care must be taken to ensure that it calls for all the information required to:

- provide evidence of the factors outlined in the person specification;
- decide whether to call the applicant for interview;
- help to structure the interview;
- take up references and check qualifications;
- form the basis for a personal employment record.

The form should also be easy for the applicant to complete. Combining the requirements of both parties takes much thought. The exact wording of questions can be important, as can the order in which the form asks them. It should also appear tidy and uncluttered, and give sufficient space for replies.

The information needed for specialist and senior posts will be more detailed than the information required for filling entry-level or unskilled posts, so it may be better to have two or three different forms for different levels of post.

However, the use of an application form has a cost. The form itself needs to be designed and printed or bought. It needs to be sent to potential candidates, some of whom will not apply, and then it needs to be processed and stored. Most forms end up being around four sides of A4 and so take time to read and assess.

Recruitment packs

These are often sent to potential applicants along with the application form and contain additional information about the job and about the employer. In highly competitive labour markets, such packs are almost akin to marketing literature as they are used to tempt candidates. Some organizations competing for high-quality and sought-after staff, such as graduates, are prepared to spend considerable sums on them.

This is not always necessary as the most important feature is that they contain the information the candidates need to know about the employer to enable them to decide whether to submit an application. Research has shown that if the candidates have good-quality information early in the recruitment and selection process, the chances of the subsequent appointment being successful are increased.

Telephone applications

There may be occasions when there is no time even for the submission of letters and CVs. In these circumstances, it may be necessary to take applications by telephone. If this is the case, it is advisable to have a form ready for the person receiving the application to complete. This will give a structure to the telephone conversation and ensure that all the necessary information is obtained from the candidate.

The spread of electronic communications will reduce the need for this method as candidates will be able easily to fax, e-mail or text their details.

Receiving and documenting applications

Each application is of the greatest importance to the applicant, so deserves care, accuracy, speed and courtesy. Above all, confidentiality should be protected.

If someone complains (as a rejected candidate may, either directly, or perhaps to the Equal Opportunities Commission, Council for Race Equality or Disability Rights Commission) it will be essential that all documents are available and in good order. Under data protection legislation, an individual may have the right to see any record containing information about him or her. You must therefore have a system to ensure that everything is received, read, registered, replied to and dealt with swiftly and carefully.

The steps to be taken include the following.

Registration and filing

Each vacancy is given a unique reference number. It can be labelled and given a date of receipt. A register can be used to record all the papers relating to it; all the subsequent actions taken; acknowledgements and other correspondence; dates of first, second and other interviews; the decision; the date the candidate was told of the result; the reply received; the taking up of references; medical examination; and joining the organization.

Acknowledgement

The practice of failing to acknowledge applications is discourteous and unprofessional. It is rightly resented by candidates and generates much ill-will for the recruiting organization.

Interview notes and test results

Some organizations use a standard format for interview notes to be completed at each interview. Regardless of whether this is used or not, good notes should be made and kept on the file.

If you use any tests or examinations (including medical examination), you will also need to record and file the results.

References

If you take up references these too will need to be registered and filed.

Monitoring and evaluation

The register will enable the process to be monitored to ensure it is progressing smoothly and on time. It can also support the evaluation of the effectiveness of recruitment methods in terms of the number of candidates attracted, time taken and costs.

All papers and records need to be kept for a period of time in case a claim of discrimination is lodged or the same post (or a similar one) falls vacant again.

The whole recruitment and selection process should be evaluated, especially if the person appointed does not fulfil expectations. Checks should be made to ensure that there is no evidence of unfair discrimination.

Selection

Selection is the stage when candidates are assessed against the person specification using the information given in their application and that learnt from other sources and at interview. The best use of the interview is the main subject of this book.

However, other sources of information may be helpful. They include selection methods such as:

- tests;
- work samples;
- portfolios of evidence;
- psychometric tests;
- reference checks.

Tests

These are most commonly used in two situations:

1. Where a basic standard (eg of literacy or numeracy) is required, and there is nothing to indicate the candidates' knowledge or ability in the area. This is most likely for entry-level posts and/ or when the candidates have no qualifications and/or recent relevant experience.
2. For higher level posts requiring creativity, literacy and the ability to conceptualize.

   If they are completed as part of the application, they can be used as a basis for choosing who to interview. However, there is no guarantee of the applicant completing the test or of him/ her doing so alone. Alternatively, the test can be done at the time of the interview and used as a basis for discussion and questioning at interview.

Work samples

These measure people's skill in performing various actions, such as driving a van or a fork-lift truck, using a computer keyboard, dealing with a typical in-tray or situation. It is essential that any test or work sample is designed to reflect the job requirements and the abilities outlined in the person specification.

Psychometric tests

Tests are available which are designed to measure psychological dimensions. The better ones are available commercially and have been extensively tested to ensure that they actually predict the criteria they claim and that they are free from discriminatory bias. These tests fall into two categories. The first comprises the tests of general intelligence (IQ = intelligence quotient). Such tests have a long history, and can give an indication of the overall intellectual abilities of candidates. These are of particular interest in the case of candidates whose educational attainments and work history may be limited.

The second group of tests includes personality tests, each of which is based on its own view of the human personality. Tests are available to measure dimensions such as introversion/extroversion, stability/instability, relaxation/tenseness and so on. Other tests take quite different approaches, depending on the particular school of thought on which they are based. Some of these tests have a long and respectable history; others may have been devised for a particular situation, or possibly, as the use of such tests has become more popular, with insufficient development. The development of the better tests will include using them on sample groups to identify the range of responses generally given.

Whatever the pedigree of the test, it is unlikely to be of help unless it is known how test performance relates to performance in the posts being filled. To demonstrate, for example, that a candidate is 'highly extrovert' does not help unless needed for effective performance and the degree of extroversion is included in the specification.

One final word of warning: when choosing and using tests, great care needs to be taken to ensure that the test, either in its format or administration, does not unfairly disadvantage a disabled person. Some tests, for example, are time limited and have very small text. This may cause someone with visual limitations undue difficulty. Some of the better publishers have produced guidelines on the appropriateness of using such tests. The way to ensure that everyone is treated fairly is to be very clear about why the test is being used and how it relates to the job, and to ask whether a candidate needs any reasonable help as a result of a disability.

Invitation to attend for interview

Once candidates have been shortlisted, they need to be told of their success and invited to attend an interview. There are distinct advantages in doing this quickly and some employers get in touch with the candidates by telephone (or even e-mail) because:

- the chances of candidates obtaining another job are reduced;
- the process is kept moving;
- the time taken to fill the post is kept to the minimum.

However, if contact is being made with candidates at their place of work, care is needed to keep their application confidential, for they may have not told their colleagues or current employer.

The initial contact should be confirmed in writing. This also allows the details of the selection process to be explained. Candidates should be told:

- the time and place of the interview;
- who will be conducting the interview;
- what should be taken to the interview (eg samples of work or a portfolio, copies of examination certificates);
- what other selection methods are to be used (with an explanation of what to expect, eg if the candidates are to give a presentation, whether an overhead projector will be available, the size of the audience, how long the presentation is to last);
- details of any tests to be completed before the interview, with instructions on how to complete the test (eg whether it is to be done alone, within a given amount of time, with or without reference to other sources of information);
- how long the interview (and other selection methods) are expected to last.

The candidates should also be asked if, owing to any disability, they need any assistance or special facilities. Also, if they are to be offered refreshments, they should be asked if they have any specific dietary considerations.

Final steps

The recruitment and selection process is not complete when a choice has been made; there are still several important tasks to be carried out. These include the following.

Making the offer of employment

After the selection panel has decided who is the best candidate an offer of employment is made. It will have been decided beforehand how to make the offer. Some employers prefer to notify all the candidates after the event, in writing. Others like to speak to the candidates either personally or on the telephone.

Whichever method is chosen, it is important to remember that the offer of employment is legally binding and should only be made by someone authorized by the organization. Timing the offer will also depend on whether the necessary checks have been completed. Even though it is possible to make the offer subject to satisfactory references, once made it can be very difficult to withdraw it.

Negotiation

Even though the candidate has been offered the job, he or she may not accept it immediately. If good quality information about the employment contract has been given early in the recruitment stages, candidates should be in no doubt about salary, terms and conditions and other benefits. However, there are certain circumstances in which these need to be negotiated with the individual who has been offered the job.

These negotiations should be held in the few days immediately following the offer. If the candidate is considering other offers, delay may be seen as incompetence or evidence of lack of commitment to the offer. Good candidates move quickly and, unless the negotiations progress, may go to another employer.

However, this does not mean that the negotiations should be carried out with undue haste. Rushing may lead to ill-considered decisions being made by both parties and lack of proper checking.

It is a regrettable fact of life that some candidates lie to get themselves a job. Therefore, reference and medical checks should be regarded as legitimate sources of information obtained as a normal part of the selection process.

References

References are useful in two ways; they can be used to cross-check what the candidate has said and they can give additional information. This should be factual, about the candidates' work history and performance, not impressions or opinions about their character.

References may be taken up (provided permission is given by the candidate) at any stage in the process, although it is usual not to take up references from the present employer until the very end in case the candidate has not told him or her about the application.

Telephone references are now more commonly used, and many recruiters believe that they are more useful than written references, as they can be obtained more quickly and there is a certainty about who is giving the reference. A pro forma should be used to structure the conversation and detailed notes taken, with the referees' knowledge. These can then be stored with the other papers.

Medical examination

It may be necessary for successful candidates to be medically examined. This is particularly important in health-related areas of work and when the candidate has direct contact with clients or customers.

Medical opinions may also be helpful to identify what aids or adjustments may be required by a disabled person or whether a candidate's health or condition may present an unacceptable risk.

Other checks

Checks should be made on employees working in certain areas (eg with children) and to ensure that an individual is eligible to work in the United Kingdom. These checks should be made before an offer of employment is made. Alternatively, a job offer can be made subject to the receipt of satisfactory replies.

Telling the unsuccessful candidates

After the offer has been made and accepted the unsuccessful candidates need to be told the sad news that their applications have not been accepted. Sometimes, if there is some doubt about the chosen candidate's acceptance, it may be better to keep one candidate in reserve until matters have been finalized. There may be a later vacancy coming up, for which an unsuccessful candidate may be suitable, so, if appropriate, offer him or her feedback on the application as a way of maintaining contact.

In all cases, you will need to treat unsuccessful candidates courteously. This is not just simple humanity, but also enlightened self-interest. The way candidates are dealt with will affect how they view the organization; they may be customers or know customers; they may be potential employees again in the future or they may obtain a job with a competitor.

Induction

The recruitment process ends when (and only when) the chosen candidate walks through the door on the appointed day, and is received happily by the work team. Inevitably, there will be certain training needs and some time will be needed as a settling-in phase. If this final stage goes wrong, all that has been done before may be wasted.

two

The **interview**

It is virtually unthinkable to fill a vacancy without one or more interviews with shortlisted candidates. However, much research has shown that unskilled interviewing is little better than tossing a coin. The way interviews are set up and conducted is important, and the questions that should be asked and the techniques used will be explored in Part 2 of this book.

The interview has distinct parts, several of which occur outside the interview-room stage and well before the interview is held. They are:

1. deciding what part the interview or interviews will play in the overall selection process;
2. designing the type of interview or interviews to be used;
3. training the interviewers;
4. preparing for the interview or interviews;
5. conducting the interview or interviews;
6. asking questions, and gathering and recording the replies and other evidence;
7. considering the evidence and other information;
8. deciding who to appoint.

The selection process

This stage starts as soon as the candidates have submitted their applications and the recruitment stage is completed. The selection process is when decisions are made about candidates' potential suitability for appointment. These decisions are improved if they are based on good-quality information gathered from a number of sources using an appropriate range of methods. The analysis of the information should be rigorous and preferably done by more than one person. In this way the chances of being able to predict which of the candidates is most likely to perform to the standard required will be increased.

Brief descriptions of some of the methods other than the interview were given in Chapter 1. These are all known to have a better ability to predict performance than the interview. Yet the interview continues to be the most widely used selection method and often the only one. Researchers suggest that this is because the interview is the only place where the candidates and employer begin to get to know each other. The social interaction and rapport are important. However, they should not be allowed to get in the way of systematically assessing the candidates' ability to do the job.

Fortunately the steps needed to improve the interview's predictive ability from the level of coin tossing are not difficult to take. The first is to agree the purpose of the interview in the selection process. Simply, its role is *to allow the exchange of information between two parties during a face-to-face meeting. This exchange is to enable both parties to make a decision about entering into a contract of employment with each other and to reduce the risk of this decision being the wrong one for either party.*

The selection process can contain several different types of interview. When the post is simple, or there are few candidates, a single round of interviews is often sufficient. For more complex or senior posts, more than one interview may be needed. The use of several stages allows the field of candidates to be reduced to a more manageable size, and using several methods allows their performance in one to be compared with performance in another. Holding several interviews also enables more individuals to be involved as interviewers. This is particularly useful when a number of individuals or departments must be satisfied.

A common pattern is: creation of shortlist; informal interviews (if used); first interviews; testing and/or work samples; carrying out checks; second interviews; final selection.

When designing the process, thought should also be given to:

■ who to involve;
■ where to hold the interviews and other activities;
■ the training needs of the interviewer/s (and others);
■ other preparation needed.

It is also important to consider how much time is being asked of the candidates, so they are not unduly inconvenienced.

Informal interviews

Informal interviews are useful when a number of similar posts are to be filled or when a shortage of suitable applicants is expected. Typically, they may help when an organization moves to a new area, mounts a major expansion programme, or during graduate recruitment. They may be combined with a display or exhibition describing and promoting the organization.

In the right situation, informal interviews can offer substantial advantages, attracting interest from potential candidates who would not otherwise apply. One drawback may include overselling of the organization or the jobs on offer, leading to waste of time at a later stage, or possibly mistaken decisions.

It should be made clear to the candidates that the purpose of the informal interview is to give them more information about the organization and that they are not being assessed.

Some organizations find that this is an opportunity to involve more people in the selection process. For example, if the post is to be part of a team and being able to form a good working relationship quickly is important, it may be appropriate to involve existing team members by asking them to meet the candidates informally.

If the informal interview is being used to assess suitability, those carrying out the assessment should be clear about the criteria they are using, for this is a time when personal bias can easily be introduced into the selection process. They also should be very aware that they have only a limited role in making the final decision and that other evidence will be used in addition to their observations.

If this form of assessment is being made, it is only fair for the candidates to be aware that they are under observation, though they need not necessarily know who is making the assessment.

Creation of the shortlist

The person specification factors should be used to accept or reject applications as they are received or when the deadline has passed. The shortlist is compiled by comparing the applications firstly against the essential specification. The list can be further reduced by comparing the applications against the desirable factors. The candidates who seem to be the closest match are invited for interview.

If the shortlist contains more than 10 candidates it may be necessary to hold preliminary tests or interviews to enable the list to be reduced further. Even at this early stage it is important to keep records summarizing the reasons for rejection.

First interviews

At the first interview the main objectives will be to sift out unsuitable candidates and gather as much relevant information as possible about the others.

Many recruiters find that at this stage a face-to-face discussion makes the establishment of rapport between candidate and interviewer easier and speeds the flow of information.

As the purpose of this interview is to gather further information, it may be acceptable for it to be conducted by a personnel professional acting on behalf of the appointing manager. However, there are dangers in one person interviewing alone. Single-handed interviewing contains a lot of scope for unintentional bias creeping in. Keeping one's personal views separate during the assessment of another person is extremely difficult, even for the most experienced interviewer. Various techniques can be used to reduce this bias, but the easiest is to obtain a second opinion.

The other danger is that you leave yourself open to accusations of unfair treatment. Having a second person present can reduce this risk, as can following a checklist containing the person specification criteria. This can be used as a structure to govern the flow of the interview, a framework against which evidence can be gathered and assessed and the basis for the interview report. This document is the record of the interview and enables the candidates to be rank ordered in terms of their closeness to the required criteria.

If the possession of technical or professional competency is included in the person specification, someone with sufficient knowledge or experience to determine the candidates' knowledge and skill should be involved as a second interviewer.

For senior appointments, the first interview may be conducted by a recruitment consultant. It is essential that the consultant understands the needs of the job thoroughly and has some insight into the organization's culture. Even so, it is better that this interview is confined to the gathering of further information. The report back to the appointing manager or managers should be a factual record of evidence showing how the candidates' experience and attainment satisfy the essential factors. This allows the managers to decide which of the candidates should be progressed to the next stages.

Using the criteria as a structure means that the interviewer can be tightly focused and time managed. As a general rule of thumb, first interviews should last around one hour. For posts demanding less experience this time can be reduced, but if it is exceeded there is a danger of gathering too much information.

A skilled interviewer is able to obtain both the *right* information and *enough* information to enable a good enough assessment of a candidate's suitability to be made. Too little information means there are gaps. The pitfall here is that assumptions are made to fill those gaps, creating incomplete stories. If too much information is gathered, the danger is that assessments are made on the basis of the quantity of evidence rather than its significance in terms of the criteria. The longer an interview goes on, the greater chance there is of repetition or overstating experiences or attainments, which, in terms of the criteria, are trivial.

Any form of interviewing is tiring as it requires concentration and the application of skills. Having a structure to follow makes it easier to focus questions as well as ensuring that all the candidates are asked about the same areas in similar ways. It helps the interviewer keep to the topic – some interviewees are also very skilful and are able to take the interview in the direction they want. Interviewees are well aware that it is their opportunity to sell themselves and will do so, given half a chance. Having a structure will help you keep to the point (and to time). Structure also helps the interviewer to listen carefully and make notes. These points are key skills you need to develop and practise.

Listening is not a passive activity. It, too, requires concentration and the use of body language and lubricators. These are the noises ('umm's and 'er's) you can use to encourage someone to keep talking.

Note-taking is essential. Sufficient evidence needs to be recorded so that later decisions are made on the basis of reality, not subjective impressions. It is well known that, on meeting a new person, you form an impression of that person from the evidence you gather during the first 60 seconds of meeting. This impression is governed by the information you already have about that person (as presented in their application or CV) and what you see of them. On the basis of the visual clues – their height, build, hairstyle, garb, jewellery, demeanour and even their use of cosmetics and perfumes – you draw conclusions about a person's role and status, socio-economic group, background and even their personality. People tend to prefer individuals they believe are similar to themselves. They also want to be around those who have comparable backgrounds and shared experiences.

The purpose of the fact-finding interview is to reduce the importance of that subjective impression and ensure that decisions are made against more explicit and objective criteria. Good interviewers are aware of their personal biases but tend to be less aware of the role played by the following, which also lead to errors of judgement:

- the first person to be interviewed makes a stronger impression than those seen later in the process;
- the last person to be interviewed retains a stronger place in the memory than those seen previously;
- a candidate who has some distinct feature or does something different sticks out in the memory more than those who conform to type.

Keeping detailed and good-quality notes helps to overcome these errors. However, taking notes can disrupt the flow of an interview. Two skills need to be developed. The first is the ability to take notes of the important factors – there is no point in having pages of irrelevant detail. The second is the ability to take notes unobtrusively. Saying this, however, most interviewees will accept that you do need to keep notes and will wait happily while you record their words.

If the interview is structured and well time managed, it is possible to conduct several in a day. The maximum number of 30-minute interviews in any one day is around six to eight candidates. At least 10 minutes needs to be allowed between each interview. This is to enable you to complete your notes and write down your overall assessment of the candidate. It will also give a little flexibility in case the interview overruns and allow you time to stretch and walk around. You also need to build in time for comfort breaks and refreshment. The first interview for more complex jobs will be longer, so the amount of time you will need in between will be greater. Therefore, the number of candidates that can be seen in any one day will be reduced.

Final selection

On the basis of the information obtained from applications or CVs and during the first interviews, you will be able to decide which of the candidates to invite to the most detailed phase of the selection process. This may comprise some of the methods described in Chapter 1 or simply a final interview.

The reasons why the candidates invited to the first interview are not being progressed should be recorded and kept on file in case there are any questions raised about the process later. Sometimes, if it proves impossible to make an appointment, you may wish to review previous decisions and possibly reconsider a candidate. Some candidates welcome feedback. If you have good records that describe how a candidate's experience, abilities and attainment were assessed against the criteria, you will be able to give feedback to unsuccessful candidates in a way that they should find constructive and uncontentious. If you are not able to answer any questions they have, candidates are more likely to be suspicious of how the decision was made. People do not like incomplete stories – they fill in the gaps for themselves and, more often than not, make the wrong assumptions.

Those candidates invited to the further stages of the selection process need to be informed as soon as possible. You may need to consider what to do if one of the candidates is not available on your preferred day. You may find that you need to be flexible about your arrangements, especially if the job is important and there are few potentially suitable candidates. This should not mean, however, that you treat one candidate any differently to the others, simply because they have an immovable appointment on the day you want to hold the interview. Some companies overcome this problem by including the dates of interviews and any other selection methods in the vacancy advertisement or recruitment information pack.

Candidates will also want to know what you intend to ask them to do. They may have special needs to be considered, such as dietary requirements if you are inviting them to dinner, or a disability that requires adjustments to be made. You are required to do this by the Disability Discrimination Act.

Second interviews

Second interviews are usually conducted by a panel, thus giving more of those involved a chance to meet the candidates, and to compare their assessments. All panel members must be clear who is in the chair, and what role they are each expected to play in the interview and the final decision. They will need full sets of documentation. They must know what has been covered in the previous stages; in particular, they must be clear how far technical competence or specialist knowledge has been explored.

A matrix is a useful device for checking that sufficient information has been gathered about a candidate and to link together that collected during the various stages of the recruitment and selection process. Table 2.1 demonstrates how such a matrix can appear.

The matrix, as well as ensuring adequate information is obtained, can be used to summarise the assessment of how well each candidate satisfies the person specification requirements. This can either be in the form of short notes or the rating score.

The following points apply to any face-to-face interview, but are particularly important during one in which appointment decisions are made.

Table 2.1 A matrix to record recruitment and selection information

Candidate . . . .

Stage Criteria	CV	References		Technical interview	Work sample	Final interview
Communications						
Decision-making						
Planning						
Technical knowledge						
Interpersonal skills						

Interview panel size and composition

Face-to-face interviewing allows rapport to be established more easily between interviewers and interviewee, and encourages a natural flow of dialogue.

However, the relationship may be damaged, because of lack of skills and experience on the part of the interviewers, or the failure to develop a rapport between candidate and interviewers. Less experienced interviewers may also find it difficult to take sufficient notes as the interview proceeds. The dangers of only one person conducting the interview have already been discussed above. Because of these, many employers make use of small panels of two or three. Frequently they will include a specialist in the relevant work and one or two generalists; perhaps a general manager and a member of the personnel function. The involvement of the manager to whom the appointed person will report is highly desirable.

To some organizations, the involvement of two or three interviewers may seem a little heavy handed, but such panels have many advantages. Each member will relate to the candidate in a different way. Members can, if they wish, adopt deliberately different approaches to the candidate and can explore different aspects of the job. It is less likely that points will be overlooked. While one member is involved in dialogue with the candidate, the others can observe, listen and take notes. Afterwards, each interviewer will be able to check and compare his or her view of the candidate against those of the others.

Occasionally, a small panel may experience some difficulty. For example, members of the panel may sometimes get in each other's way, either duplicating lines of questioning or missing areas out on the assumption others will cover them. They may fail to understand each other's methods, interrupting, interpreting or even answering a colleague's questions. Tensions may exist between panel members, and an over-dominant member may distort the result. However, thorough training and preparation usually prevent these difficulties from arising.

Large panels with six and more members enable many people to be involved in the selection. Membership of such panels is usually driven by the organization's need to be seen to involve certain individuals in the decisions. It may also be influenced by the importance of involving certain interest factions in the assessment of the candidates' suitability, for example if the role holder will be working across departments, functions or different teams.

The disadvantages of large panels arise from their clumsiness. It will be difficult for panel members to establish rapport with the candidate, or to pursue a consistent line of questioning. Political factors (with a large or small 'p') may make control difficult, and not all members may get a fair chance to ask questions. The procedure is loaded against candidates who do not enjoy public performance, even though this skill may not figure on the person profile. Group dynamics between panel members may get in the way of the real purpose of the interview. Again, good preparation can help to avoid this. The role of the interview chair is essential in managing the panel and keeping members focused on the task of assessing each candidate thoroughly and fairly.

As large panels can be difficult to control and may act as unnecessary obstacles to candidates, it may be better to find other ways to involve people who need to be part of the process. *Group interviews or discussions* in which a number of candidates will be watched by a panel of observers are sometimes used. The technique is most useful in exploring the social and interpersonal skills of candidates, and may also be used to test leadership skills.

The need to have all candidates present at the same time and to keep them until other elements of the process (such as individual interviews) have been completed may cause difficulties. For this reason, the technique is most commonly used when a number of similar posts are being filled at the same time, as with graduate intakes or as part of an assessment centre.

Peer group interviewing or *specific topic interviews*, in which the panel is made up of potential colleagues or other people with legitimate contributions to make are less usual but interesting variants. These allow specific aspects of the person specification to be explored in more depth, for example teamworking approaches, technical knowledge or professional competence can be assessed. These will usually be combined with more conventional interviews.

If peer group interviewing is not used, there should at least be an opportunity for candidates to tour the work environment and meet those who may become their colleagues.

How these secondary interviews are to report back to the appointment panel needs to be decided beforehand. You should also be very clear about how opinions will be used when the final decision is being made.

The environment

Where an interview is held can have a surprising effect on its degree of success. The most skilful interviewing techniques will achieve little if deployed in an atmosphere of distractions and interruptions.

The aspects of the environment that matter most are:

- the reception arrangements;
- the interview room;
- furniture.

Reception arrangements are improved if security and reception staff have been alerted to the candidates' expected arrival.

A decent waiting room, or at least a comfortable chair in the secretary's office is needed. A choice of reading matter is welcome and can be useful, for example brochures or information about the organization and its work, as well as appropriate journals or newspapers, will help to occupy the waiting candidate.

The candidates can be asked to fill in their expense claims or complete a standard personal data form if the application was made by letter or CV. It is courtesy to offer the candidate a drink of tea or coffee, a soft drink or water and the use of the cloakroom facilities before they go in to meet the interviewers.

The interview room must be private, free from interruption and distraction, and reasonably tidy and comfortable. Most organizations have suitable accommodation such as committee, meeting or board rooms, or even special interview rooms. If you need to use your office, you may wish to give some thought to its layout, which can affect the atmosphere of the interview.

The furniture and the way it is arranged can do a lot to establish the atmosphere. Conducting an interview across a desk, especially your own, conveys a feeling of status, and the physical barrier will create a psychological barrier which makes rapport harder to establish. Piles of work and objects are distracting, and can make an interviewee feel as though more important tasks are being interrupted.

In addition to the impact that the position of the furniture may have on the flow of the interview, the type of furniture also deserves some consideration. It may seem friendly to position low, soft chairs around a coffee table. However, to someone with back problems, such seating arrangements could cause significant difficulties. You also need to remember that interviewers will need to consult papers and make notes. Clipboards may satisfy this need but they tend to be clumsy. You may find it easier to sit at a table of the correct height.

Given the requirements of the Disability Discrimination Act, it may be better to keep matters simple and make use of ordinary (usually well-designed) office chairs and place them around an empty table or desk. A confrontational layout should be avoided by, for example, using a round table or by placing interviewers on three sides.

The overall layout of the room can have an impact on the candidate. For example, placing the interviewers in front of a window can mean that the candidate is unable to see the interviewers' faces. This can make it difficult for the interviewee to assess the impact of his or her answers. For those with hearing difficulties who rely on lip-reading to 'hear' what is being said, it can lead to considerable disadvantage.

Preparing for the interview

Lack of preparation is one of the biggest causes of ineffective interviewing. However experienced you are, it is impossible to interview effectively unless you have obtained as much information as you can about each candidate and planned your strategy before you meet them. The initial interview plan should focus on the person specification. Questions should be designed to elicit information from the applicants in a way that supplies the interviewers with the evidence they need to assess how well each matches the required criteria. Generally, this is done by starting with low-level questions – opening, easy-to-answer questions designed to settle the applicant into the interview. These are followed by more probing questions aimed at gaining the necessary information.

The general questions should be asked of all of the candidates in a similar fashion to ensure that the evidence needed is obtained in a consistent way. However, they will need to be augmented by questions specific to each applicant, which come from the information given in the application or on the CV.

The interviewers should be involved in the development of the questions. This gives them insight into the whole process and enables them to understand the criteria being used for assessment. They can decide who is going to ask which question and plan the overall flow of the interview. This process can been seen as having four parts:

- ▧ **Welcome**, during which the applicants are settled in.
- ▧ **Acquiring** information from the applicants.
- ▧ **Supplied** information to the applicants about the job and organization.
- ▧ **Parting**, when the applicants are asked whether they are still firm candidates.

The mnemonic 'WASP' will help you keep this in mind.

All interviewers should familiarize themselves with the candidates' applications in three stages. The first stage will take place during shortlisting, to allow time for necessary research and thought. The second stage will be undertaken 24 hours or so before the interview, and the final stage will be a quick refresher immediately before meeting the candidate.

During the *first stage*, the interviewers will consider each application individually in relation to the person specification. Once the applications to be progressed have been established, it is useful to highlight information that seems significant or needs probing further. This can result in a list of questions that need to be posed to an individual candidate to supplement those asked to all. It is also useful to identify gaps in the information or aspects that need to be checked, for example regarding previous work history. Interviewers may list questions or areas of interest that need exploration. They may conduct research of their own, either to check statements made (if possible) or to ensure there is sufficient background.

In the *second stage*, the interviewer re-reads each application and thinks of the series as a whole rather than only of each individual candidate.

The *third stage*, immediately before meeting the candidate, ensures that the interviewer has fresh information about the candidate, including name, present situation, place of residence, and any points from the application that need more exploration.

The interview itself

The three levels

The interview is in some ways a false situation in which both parties play parts on at least three levels.

At the *first level*, both are likely to pay lip service to the two-way nature of what they are doing. The interviewers will claim that they are anxious to give all the information to the applicant that the latter wants, that they are being scrupulously fair, that the applicants will have every opportunity to present themselves in the best possible way, and so on.

The applicants will make out that they are being honest, truthful and open in all that is said, and that their only desire is to prove to the interviewers' satisfaction that they are really the best choice for the post.

At the *second level*, both parties will know that while the employer alone can offer or withhold the job, the applicant can decide whether to accept or reject the offer.

The interviewers should regard everything said by the applicants with caution, unless and until the applicants have established themselves as credible. Even then, some healthy doubt should remain.

Applicants will do all they can to sell themselves. This may include bending the truth to their own advantage, hiding problems, and playing up good points. Applicants have been known to lie about material facts.

At the *third level*, both parties will realize that a mistake in what is being done would have serious, long-term consequences for both, that job selection is difficult, and that they would do well to help themselves by helping each other.

It is at this third level that both interviewers and candidates need to operate, but getting and staying there demands much understanding and will-power, for in effect the interview is a negotiation about a high-value contract.

Style

The interview has been defined as 'a conversation with a purpose', but this begs an important question: is it a real dialogue aimed at setting up a real relationship, or is the situation purely conventional, with strict limits and detachment on both sides?

If *genuine dialogue* is used, the aim is to use the interview as the start of a potential relationship which may subsequently grow. Because you are meeting someone who may work with you, your aim will be to lay the best foundations you can for a long-term, worthwhile relationship. The relationship may not, of course, develop, as either party may abort the process, but at this stage you do not know.

This approach to the negotiation can be seen as a sort of courtship. Both parties will put themselves forward in the best light, but without deception which might later jeopardize the relationship. Both will give of their personality, and seek to learn about the other. When subjects are discussed, real opinions will be exchanged, and a rapport may develop. If difficulties are encountered, they will be talked through openly and constructively. Both parties will be prepared to adapt during the course of the interview. Both will develop a sense of obligation to the other for what has passed between them. Both will seek mutual satisfaction from the relationship.

To work, this approach to interviewing must be consistent both with the style of the organization and the personality of the interviewers. The organization must be open and flexible, and the interviewers must be secure, mature and prepared.

The style is frequently used by selection consultants and headhunters, most of whom, while working for a client who pays them, feel the need to operate as an 'honest broker'.

In *conventional interviewing*, the interviewers deliberately maintain a distance from the interviewees. No relationship is developed, and if any appears to be growing it is consciously suppressed. When subjects are discussed, the interviewers withhold their own views. The interview is bound by conventions which set it apart from a normal social situation; what happens in the interview room is separate from everything that happens outside.

This style of interviewing is appropriate for organizations with a rigid structure and a hierarchical management style.

It is not necessarily wrong or inappropriate. If the management style of the organization is like this, it would be wrong to portray it as otherwise to applicants.

Stress interviewing is occasionally used. The term describes an interview in which interviewees are put under deliberate pressure by the type of questions asked or the manner of their being asked.

Questions may be specifically aimed at areas of apparent problems, weaknesses or embarrassment, or they may be deliberately phrased to offend to test how the applicants react.

Occasionally, sadistic or unskilled interviewers will adopt such an approach, justifying it, if at all, with the belief that they learn 'what someone is made of' by how they respond. Most experienced interviewers feel, however, that for every piece of relevant information thrown up during such an interview there will be many more that are lost because of the defensiveness, hostility and lack of rapport that it produces.

The person specification may occasionally include factors which justify this approach; an ability to put up with personal insults from strangers being the most obvious. Such requirements are rare, and the need for 'stress interviewing' is usually unjustified.

Keep control. Whatever style is adopted, the interviewers must retain control of the interview.

Interviews should achieve the objectives both of interviewers and interviewees. But it must rest with one party to establish and maintain control of the proceedings; if both try, the interview will rapidly lose focus. There is a similar danger of the interviewers engaging in a power struggle, though good training and preparation should avoid this. The person leading the interview has ultimate responsibility for controlling its flow and should therefore manage its dynamics.

Who does the talking? In any interview, the interviewees should do most of the talking. No exact proportion is right or wrong, but a guide figure of 80 per cent interviewees and 20 per cent interviewers is usually not far out. The interviewers will have more to say during the welcome phase and in response to any questions raised by the interviewees.

The phases of the interview

As mentioned earlier, there are four basic phases:

- welcome;
- acquisition;
- supply;
- parting.

Each of these is described in more detail in the chapters that follow.

The *welcome* will include greeting the interviewee, personal introductions, and clarification as to how much is known about the organization and the post to be filled. The interviewers will try to relax the interviewees, establish rapport, and set up a natural conversational flow. It is *not* an objective of this phase to assess the interviewees on the basis of first impressions. Any temptation to do so should be firmly resisted.

The *acquisition* phase is carried out using *methodical questioning* and will usually constitute the bulk of the interview. Based on a clear plan, it will aim to explore each interviewee's past, present and future and their relevance to the post to be filled.

The *supply* phase will offer the interviewee a chance to clear up doubts and make any final points. This is the stage at which the interviewees make sure that they have enough information on which to base their decision should they be offered the job.

The *parting* is used to ensure the interviewees are still interested in the post and to inform them what will happen next. Generally, this includes when the decision will be made, how they will be notified and what, if any, arrangements will be made to provide feedback for the interviewees.

Note-taking

It is not possible to retain everything of significance that is said during even the shortest of selection interviews. The human brain is far less able to retain everything that passes during long, in-depth ones.

Even those gifted with the most exceptional powers of memory would be unable to select those passages during an interview which only subsequent events might render significant; statements, for example, which later replies indicated needed probing, or with which the claims of later candidates might need comparison. In a long series of interviews, you may confuse and forget interviewees, let alone what they said or did.

Effective interviewing therefore calls for every aid to memory that can sensibly be used. Audio or video recording are occasionally used, although many interviewers reject them on the grounds that they would make interviewees (not to mention most interviewers) tense and artificial, and that the time required to analyse replays would be at least as long as the interview itself.

Inevitably, the interviewers are thrown back on the need to make comprehensive notes. This is not easy, and needs practice and the right approach.

Permission

Some interviewers prefer to ask interviewees' permission to take notes, or at least draw their attention to the fact that this is to happen. Most interviewees expect notes to be taken, and if they have feelings on the subject will almost certainly see it as fair and professional.

Some interviewees may take their own notes during the interview, or may refer to notes prepared before the interview.

Volume of notes

It is difficult to predict what may prove to be important, so it is best to take quite full notes. This does not mean trying to create a verbatim record; rather make concise notes of key points.

You must not allow your note-taking to hinder the establishment of rapport and the flow of information. The practised interviewer is able to make notes unobtrusively. In any case, as interviewees are aware of what you are doing, there is no harm in pausing to complete the note before moving on to the next topic.

Use quotes

There is a danger that, in summarizing or editing replies, you introduce unconscious bias. The nearer your notes can be to what is actually said, the better. You should try to write down replies which seem important in the exact words used.

Observations

You should also keep a note of how the interviewees presented themselves and any particular patterns of behaviour. However, you need to take care not to make assumptions. For example, rather than recording 'appeared nervous', you should note 'shuffled in chair when asked about. . .'

Timing

When you make a note can affect the interview.

If you are finding it difficult to get the flow going, it is best to postpone note-taking until things are easier.

The interviewee will probably spot the point at which you write a note, and may try to guess what has been written and why. If the interviewee is giving straightforward information, this will not matter, but if less than honest replies are being given, the interviewee may be a little concerned about the fact that a record is being kept.

Writing up

At the end of each interview, before seeing the next candidate, you will need to review your notes to make sure you have included any points not noted during the interview. You will need to check that they say what you intended. This is also the time to record your overall assessment of the candidate while he or she is still fresh in your mind.

Some organizations find it helpful to provide pro-forma interview record forms and may include the person specification criteria to aid assessment.

Interpretation and decision-making

The temptation to make judgements on candidates at the end of each interview is very great, but you should try to avoid doing so. Each candidate will make an impression on you, even when you are using strict criteria, and the trap is to believe that the last candidate is the perfect person or totally unappointable. . . but wait until you see the next.

The time for overall conclusions is at the end of the series of interviews, when all the candidates have been seen. This is when your notes will come into their own. They will provide the information to enable you to assess each candidate against the criteria and to compare your assessment with those made by the other interviewers.

The normal procedure is for the interviewers to decide if there is total agreement about any candidate's total unsuitability for the post. If there is unanimous agreement, this candidate can be discounted from further consideration. If not, all the candidates are considered in turn, usually in the order of the interview sequence. This helps the interviewers to recall the candidates.

Traps to avoid

When considering interviewees, there are several traps to avoid.

Primacy and *recency*. The panel may remember the interviewees seen at the beginning and end of the sequence, and over-value their claims, particularly if the series has been long.

Skilled presentation. Interviewees who have presented themselves outstandingly well will be prominent in the interviewers' thinking, at the expense of the less articulate. If self-presentation figures on the person specification, this is valid, but if not it should not be allowed to influence the decision.

Domination. The interviewers may be dominated by one or two of their number, who may try to steamroller the others into a decision with which they do not really agree. This is specially likely if it is the most senior member who holds strong views. The person responsible for the interview should chair the meeting in a way that avoids such inappropriate pressure.

Lack of process. Many interview panels have no systematic approach to making a collective decision, and without one the discussion can be unfocused, irrational and repetitive. To ensure the decision-making is based on the evidence gathered during each stage and is justifiable, a clear and understood process is essential, and it is worth spending time agreeing this during the preparation stage. A decision-making process which many panels have found useful is given next.

A decision-making process

There are three stages:

1. A last check should be made, in the light of all the information available, that each interviewee meets the essential criteria

outlined in the person specification. Any who do not must be finally eliminated.

2. A comparison should be made of all remaining interviewees against the criteria. This process will be easier if a matrix such as that shown in Table 2.1 is used, with each column devoted to an interviewee, and each row to a criterion. The rankings are then totalled for each candidate. The one with the highest total will be the one who appears to meet the criteria best, and will be the provisional choice.

3. The evidence for the provisional choice should now be reviewed, asking the questions:
   - 'Does this choice seem sensible in the light of each aspect of the evidence?'; and
   - 'If we appointed this person, what can we foresee that might go wrong?'

Sometimes it is useful to rate the interviewees' suitability for appointment on an overall rating scale, such as the one given below:

1 = totally unappointable
2 = doubtful
3 = possible
4 = likely
5 = definitely appointable

If an overall ranking scale such as this is used, the reasons for allocating a rating should be recorded.

An interview panel may find it helpful to use a flipchart to record the assessment of each interviewee. This enables the ratings, either by the person specification or on the overall scale, to be clearly visible to all interviewers. The use of a flipchart focuses attention on the criteria and helps to reduce the introduction of irrelevant factors. It keeps consideration of the interviewees to the point and thus enables the decisions to be made in a structured fashion.

Upon telling interviewees when the decision will be announced, care should be taken to avoid putting undue pressure on the interview panel. Considering the interviewees in turn does take time, and the time needed will be influenced by the number of panel members and interviewees. It may be fairer to tell the interviewees that they will be contacted the following day rather than rushing into making hasty decisions. The old saying 'marry at haste; repent at leisure' applies equally well to appointment decisions made without due consideration.

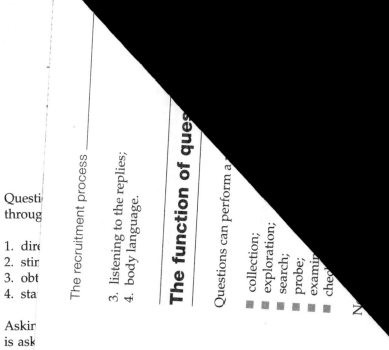

Questi
throug

1. dir
2. stir
3. obt
4. sta

Askir
is ask
not fi

recorded and interpreted. Depending ...
your following questions may be modified. Questioning is an interactive, dynamic process.

The physical environment and emotional atmosphere in which a question is asked will affect the way it is heard by the candidate, and the response it produces. The simplest question, such as:

☐ **Are you sure?**

will not sound the same in the torture chamber as in the office of a positive and supportive interviewer.

The atmosphere will be the product of many factors, including the room layout, the style of the interview, the sequence of questions and the tone of voice and body language of the interviewers. The importance of layout, furniture and style were discussed in Chapter 2. Sequence and body language are discussed below.

Using questions effectively is an art and, like other arts, it can be improved through thought, study and practice. Asking questions can be divided into four headings:

1. the function of questions;
2. the types of question;

number of functions. These include:

ation (if used);
k (if needed).

order is always right. You must be flexible and ready to change your approach according to circumstances. But as part of your preparation for the interview, you may plan to move through a logical sequence such as that given in the following subsections.

Collection

This aims to clear the ground by filling any gaps in your knowledge of the candidate's background. These might exist because the CV supplied by the candidate omitted something, because a section of the application form had not been fully completed, or because a subject did not seem to have been covered at a previous interview.

Collecting questions will be of the closed or the yes/no type.

If, for example, you are seeking information about the candidate's current job, you might ask:

☐ Do you report directly to the purchasing manager, or is there a section head between you?
☐ Can you please confirm the date you were appointed to the post you currently hold?

Exploration

Exploration begins with the definition of the area to be explored, and goes on to discover and describe everything you can find out about that area.

In selection interviewing, exploration will often be the first approach, both to gaining information about each candidate as an individual person and to specific topics. You may begin with a general examination of the candidate's CV. Later in the interview, you may wish to obtain detailed information about a particular time in the candidate's working life. What, for example, was the candidate responsible for, and what was achieved?

The questions used during exploration will usually be open-ended. However, it can be productive to use a mixture of open and closed, even open and yes/no questions.

For the candidate's current job, you might ask:

☐ **Can you summarize for me your main duties?** (Open to start the flow.)
☐ **Looking back, do you feel this job has really prepared you to move on?** (Yes/no question to focus the thinking and invite comment.)
☐ **Why do you say that?** (Follow-up open question.)

Search

Searching differs from exploration in that you know what you are looking for, and that the answer is there somewhere. Your chances of finding whatever it is will be improved if you are able to define the search more tightly.

In a selection interview, the purpose of such a search is to obtain relevant information that may not be immediately known by the candidate, for example his or her long-term ambitions, the reasons why a particular course of action was taken, or why new jobs were pursued.

The type of question used will vary according to whether the interviewer believes the information sought is consciously available to the candidate. If the candidate is genuinely unsure, either through lack of insight or fault of memory, the questioner may use open, followed by closed questions. If the candidate is likely to know the answer, the immediate question may be closed or yes/no.

Typical questions might be:

☐ **How did you get your ideas accepted as a junior member of the team?** (Focusing the thinking with an open question)

☐ **Was your solution actually implemented?** (Yes/no, assuming the candidate is likely to know, or perhaps the previous question helped to recall the incident)

Probe

This is one of the interviewer's most powerful weapons. It is used when you are unsure whether what you have heard is correct or you need more information. The aim of the probe is, as its name implies, to dig deeper.

This does not necessarily imply deceit on the part of the candidate. Candidates often make mistakes from nerves, failings of memory, failure to express themselves well, or because they are unsure of the answers sought by the questioner; good interviewing often helps the candidates to express themselves more easily. Sometimes, the interviewers may simply not hear or understand what is said, or may not have been able to record all of the answer. You must be careful that in probing you do as little as possible to destroy the rapport that has been built up, and approach your probe so that you do not appear excessively interrogative.

The probe may be needed at any time. If you are satisfied that what you have been told gives you what you wanted, there will be nothing to probe. Likewise, you may wish to pass over unimportant matters, even though the answers may be incomplete. On important matters, however, you may have to probe and take time to get the information you need.

More interviews go wrong from a lack of probing than from too much. Inexperienced interviewers may be nervous of using the probe question, but it is a legitimate tool and should be used when needed without hesitation.

There is no set form for a probe; it may be used as part of any type of question. Typical probes might be:

☐ **You mentioned your section leader earlier; how did she react when you approached your manager directly on this project?**
☐ **I was particularly interested in your use of regression analysis for this application. Trying hard to remember my elementary statistics, I'm not sure how I could do that. Can you enlighten me?**
☐ **What savings did all this actually produce?**
☐ **Does that mean that one of your colleagues lost his or her job?**

Examination

Examination differs from probing in that both the questioner and the responder believe that the questioner knows the correct answer. It is also a powerful technique for use when the interviewer suspects that the candidate is withholding needed information or trying to conceal details, such as the fact that the individual was a *member* of a successful team, not its leader, as implied. The technique is also useful for checking levels of technical or professional knowledge. Some candidates are experienced interviewees, and know the techniques better than many interviewers. If you suspect you are interviewing such a candidate, you should be prepared to be thorough in your examination of his or her claimed experience and achievements.

Check

A check aims to ensure that you have heard and understood the reply to a previous question correctly. It can follow any other type of question.

Its use may interrupt the flow, and occasionally harm rapport, so it should not be used more often than really necessary. However, it is even more harmful to mishear an important answer. If you feel it is necessary, you may offer a brief apology, but accuracy is so clearly in the interests of the candidate that few will object.

The most effective check is to restate what you thought you heard. But you must do this without any comment, even implied by your tone of voice, to avoid planting doubts in the candidate's mind which might lead to the reply being altered.

You might ask:

☐ I see. You are saying that your manager found it easier to work with you directly because your section leader lacked experience in this particular area? or

☐ Thank you. Your point, if I have grasped it correctly, is that the savings were available, but never actually made, as management were anxious to avoid disrupting a long-standing relationship with a particular supplier?

An alternative method of checking is simply to ask the same questions again, after a suitable lapse of time. The candidate may point out that the question has been asked before, in which case you may wish to apologize briefly yet await the second reply.

The types of question

Questions belong to one of several types, depending on the way they are asked. They are often classified as:

- the open question;
- the closed question;
- the yes/no question;
- the multiple question;
- the leading question.

The open question

This is a question which indicates an area of interest, but allows a range of possible replies. It is particularly valuable when *exploring* and *searching* for information about a topic, but not appropriate when *collecting* or *examining* facts. It may or may not be suitable for the process of *probing* a specific subject.

For example, it can be used to explore a candidate's response or approach to dealing with a difficulty such as a bad examination result:

☐ **How did you feel about that?**

In exploring social skills, you may ask:

☐ **What approaches did you find worked best in this kind of situation?**

Considering problem-solving skills, you may ask:

☐ **What was your thinking in those circumstances?**

The degree of openness can vary widely. At one end of the scale, you might consider starting an interview by asking a question such as:

☐ **Tell me about yourself**

offering the broadest possible latitude. At the other end of the scale, you may simply ask a question of the form:

☐ **Why did you do that?**

The more open the question, the more appropriate it is for the early, exploratory stage of the interview, or of a particular topic.

An open question can rarely, except as an admission of a serious lapse of memory or lack of knowledge, be answered *'I don't know'*.

Open questions often (but not always) begin with 'How', 'Why' or 'Tell me about. . .'

The closed question

Closed questions channel the reply towards a precisely defined area. They are the right type for *collecting* and *examining* facts and details. They may be suitable for *probing*, occasionally for *searching*, but never for *exploring*.

You may ask, for example:

☐ **What salary did they give you when you were appointed to that post?**
☐ **How long did you do that job?** or
☐ **Who did you report to at that time?**

Closed questions frequently begin with 'Who', 'What', 'When', 'Where' or phrases like 'How much', 'How many', or 'How long'.

The yes/no question

Yes/no questions are closed questions that, as the name implies, call only for the answer 'Yes' or 'No'. They are ideal for *collecting*, and may be used for *examining* and *probing* information, but are quite unsuitable for *exploring* background details or reasons.

You may need to ask, for example:

☐ **Did you have a car with that job?**
☐ **Are you prepared to travel abroad?** or
☐ **Have you used online data exchange?**

In practice, many candidates tend to enlarge on their yes/no answer, as not qualifying or explaining a reply is generally seen in a poor light.

The multiple question

A multiple question has two or more parts:

☐ **Please tell me about your main achievements in your current job. How did you achieve them, and what skills relevant to the present job have you developed?**

Such questions usually confuse the interviewee, and are rarely effective. You should split them into their constituent parts and ask each separately.

The leading question

A leading question tries to guide the candidate towards or away from a particular answer.

You may ask:

☐ **Were you surprised by the result?**
☐ **Did you find the lack of support hard to deal with?**
☐ **That must have been very difficult; did you ask for help?**

Leading questions indicate the attitude of the interviewer and point to the hoped-for reply, and can produce the sought-after answers rather than the candidate's true views. On the other hand, they can be valuable as a means of confirming details. The interviewer needs to phrase the question carefully and be prepared to check if there is any doubt about the truth of the reply.

Leading questions frequently, but not always, end with an additional phrase such as 'did you?', 'were you?', 'could you?' etc. They may contain judgemental words: 'bad', 'good', 'successful' etc. They may use an apparently open question or statement which is turned into a leading question by the tone of voice:

☐ **And that was the end of the matter?**

Repetition and rephrasing

At any stage, the candidate may fail to understand the question. This may result from poor phrasing or simple inaudibility. The candidate may fail to listen fully, be confused by nerves or not understand what has been asked

You will first need to realize what is happening. If there is a deafening silence, or the candidate asks you to repeat the question, this may not be too difficult. More frequently, however, the candidate will try to make the best of a bad job, afraid of appearing stupid by admitting to being puzzled, and you will need to be sufficiently alert to pick up the situation quickly.

Having done this, you have a number of strategies to choose from. You can:

- interrupt and repeat your question;
- interrupt and rephrase your question;
- interrupt and ask a different question;
- listen to what is being said, then repeat or rephrase the question when the candidate has finished;
- listen to what is being said, deciding why the mistake was made, what that adds to your knowledge of the candidate, and whether it opens a new line of questioning.

Which you choose will depend on the importance of the original question, the apparent significance of the error, your interest in what is being said, and the time available. Most interviewers will listen at least for a short time to be sure the candidate is not going to answer the question, before deciding which action to take.

Listening to the replies

There is no point in asking effective questions if you do not listen to the replies.

There are a number of aids to help you listen more effectively. They include:

- active listening;
- avoiding preconceptions;
- 'hearing between the lines';
- summary and restatement.

Active listening

Listening must both be active and be seen to be active.

Your concentration will be improved if you watch the speaker, note the body language, and maintain good (but not absolutely continuous or frighteningly intense) eye contact.

To be seen to be listening actively, you should adopt an alert posture and expression, and react with appropriate nods, facial expressions, occasional encouraging noises and brief statements: 'I see', 'Right', 'Go on', 'Really!'.

With some candidates, you may need to staunch their flow. In this case, your listening activities will be different. You may stop taking notes, glance pointedly at your papers, withhold noises of encouragement, and break in to refocus the interview back to your prepared plan, but you should never be rude.

Avoiding preconceptions

It is difficult to avoid preconceptions, but you should at least be aware of your own, and the influence they have on your decisions.

Research suggests that many interviewers judge candidates within the first two minutes of an interview, often by irrelevancies such as the way they walk across the room, the strength of their handshake, whether they sit before being asked, or similar patterns of behaviour. Having formed such first impressions, they use the remainder of the interview to support their judgement, picking out replies that support the belief they have formed, and ignoring, forgetting or mishearing those that go against it.

Everyone tends to interpret identical patterns of behaviour according to their own system of beliefs and values. These are based on attitudes, experiences and prejudices. No one is free from these, so every judgement is made from a personal, subjective point of view.

There is also a tendency to make decisions on the basis of association. Thus, if the interviewer believes the candidate to be clever, he or she will interpret a long hesitation before answering a question as proof of careful evaluation of the question and in-depth consideration of the best possible reply. But if the interviewer believes the candidate to be stupid, the same hesitation will be seen as a lack of understanding and a slow mental reaction.

A witty reply by a candidate liked by the interviewer will be seen as an indication of his or her friendly and outgoing disposition; but the same response by a candidate who is distrusted will be regarded as uncalled-for cheek.

This is known as the 'halo and horns' effect. If you find a feature in a candidate that you like, there is a danger that you will assume that everything about the candidate is likeable and positive, ie he or she can do no wrong. Similarly, if a candidate says or does something you do not like, does not say or do something you expected or disagrees with you on something, you may assume everything about the candidate is damnable.

Basically, everyone likes to be surrounded by people they like and who are like themselves. This is achieved by the use of mental short cuts that enable assumptions to be made and conclusions to be formed without having to do a great deal of work. These mental short cuts were developed to enable us to sum up situations and react quickly in the face of potential danger. While they may have had value in the past, they can be a problem in selection interviewing. You may find that your mental short cuts have led you towards discounting candidates on grounds unconnected with their ability to do the job.

Indeed, many suitable candidates have been rejected because early failure during the interview has blinded interviewers to later and stronger indications of achievement and potential.

The point goes deeper than saying that everyone tends to judge others on the basis of slim and irrelevant evidence. This may be true, but even worse, there is a very real danger of hearing replies wrongly. Let interviewers beware!

The way to avoid the trap is to be aware first of the dangers of initial impressions and the fact that mental short cuts can lead to assumptions and prejudgements, and second of your own personal preferences, which may blind you when assessing other people. The best way is to use a checklist of criteria to ensure that you gather evidence during the whole of the interview and to resist the temptation of forming conclusions too soon.

'Hearing between the lines'

In the story of Silver Blaze, Sherlock Holmes solves a mystery by noting that a dog did not bark in the night (thus proving that the crime was committed by its owner). When attempting to interpret written material such as references and testimonials, it is essential to note not only the positive statements that are made about the candidate, but to spot the gaps – the things that might be expected, but are not there.

The same applies during an interview. Hearing what is not said, but might have been, may be as important as hearing what is said.

Failure to say something may arise from innocent causes. The fault may be yours; perhaps you have asked an involved or multiple question which confused the candidate.

On the other hand, it may be a deliberate evasion of a problem area, or perhaps an attempt to draw the discussion on to more favourable ground for the candidate:

☐ **Was it your decision to leave Smith Ltd in 1998, or did they ask you to leave?**

I got more and more fed up with the way they were treating me at Smith's. My boss was a thoroughly self-centred man, who was forever creeping to the directors. I felt the time had come for me to look around and work out what I really wanted from life. I had never made use of my training as a typesetter, and it seemed to me that was the way forward for me. I started looking for ways I could use my skill and get job satisfaction. I knew I was a first-rate printer.

You still do not know the answer.

Gaps in what is said are frequently less obvious, and not necessarily a direct failure to answer a question:

☐ **Tell me about your time with Brown Bros.**

I enjoyed it a lot. They were terrific people there; a real good crowd. Everyone used to muck in, and we'd spend time together after work. The managers were the same – no class distinction there, no status symbols. I still keep up with most of them, even now. . .

And the work?

Summary and restatement

The act of retelling what has been said, either in the same words or, more usually, in summary, is a useful aid to effective listening. Not only does this provide a check when there is any doubt, but it helps to discipline interviewers by requiring them to show that they have heard and understood.

It is, of course, unnecessary to repeat or summarize every answer; you should only do so when doubt remains in an important area or you need to indicate that you are moving on to a new area.

Body language

Everyone sends out messages through their use of body language all the time; you cannot avoid doing so. Your body reflects your feelings. There is nothing special about this; it is obvious when someone is looking bored, tired or embarrassed. It is easy to tell from posture or small movements of the hands, fingers or lower limbs whether someone is showing impatience or tension. Everyone can spot and interpret the blush.

The effective interviewer will pay particular attention to body language.

The body speaks louder than the voice

If the language of the rest of the body appears to contradict what the mouth is saying you should not believe the mouth.

Language is the most sophisticated product of the human intellect, and much effort is spent in refining and controlling its use. The rest of the body is a complex, yet comparatively primitive entity, over which only partial control can be exercised. If behaviour indicates something different from the words spoken, it is virtually certain to be nearer to the truth.

The interviewer must learn to look closely for signs of unexpected tension or other spontaneous reactions when interviewing. You will rarely see the candidate actually squirm when you probe a particular point, but you may well observe signs that may suggest tension or anxiety in the hands or eyes, or by a shift of posture.

If the candidate expresses keen interest in some aspect of the job, or agrees with a statement you make, you should watch to see if posture and expression tell the same story.

However, you should be careful not to make assumptions. For example, if a candidate taps his or her feet while you are explaining an aspect of the job to them, it does not necessarily mean that he or she is bored or impatient. It could mean that pins and needles have set in. Or if the candidate scratches their nose while answering your question about why he or she left a previous job, it does not always indicate a lie, possibly just a tickle.

If the body language shown by the candidate does not match what is being said, or the candidate is demonstrating signs that cause you some concern, you should use probing questions to gather more information. It is unwise to make assumptions about motives or state of mind simply on the evidence of your eyes.

Use your own body language effectively

To be fully effective as an interviewer, you will need to ensure that your own body reinforces the message you wish to send, and does not contradict or overlay it with another message.

If you wish to appear interested and alert, for example, you must suppress the bodily signs of tiredness and boredom. If you wish to seem friendly and cooperative, you will suppress the spontaneous bodily reactions of disagreement, disbelief and aggression.

In interviewing, your aim will be to encourage the candidate to talk freely, especially during the early phases or if there appear to be difficulties. Body language will be of great help in this, just as it will help to silence a candidate who is going on too long.

You will often wish to suppress your reactions to answers. If you show that you think a reply is good, you may spark off a stream of similar but insincere responses; if you show your dislike of something, the alert candidate will rapidly adjust all future answers.

Learn to observe and interpret the body language of others better

Everyone notices and interprets body language naturally. Some are more aware than others, to such an extent that they may find it difficult to continue a normal conversation with someone whose body language indicates complete dislike of the other person. Some people are unaware of such messages, and find themselves continually surprised when others react in a way they did not anticipate.

As with the spoken word, everyone can improve sensitivity to body language by study, thought, and observation. First become conscious of the subject and make the most of your opportunities for observation and practice day by day. You can cross-check your reading of other people's body language by asking them questions. Doing this outside the interview setting gives you the chance to test your reading of the other person's body language without the pressure of having to make a decision. In panel interviews you can discuss your observations with other panel members at the end of the interview.

Note-taking and keeping records

It is essential that you keep notes of the answers given to your questions. If you have asked any questions in addition to those planned in advance of the interview, you should also keep a note of these. Your records need not be a verbatim account of every word spoken. But you should ensure that you have recorded the main points of the answer. You will need these notes later to help you recall exactly what the candidate said and to help you form your assessment at the end of the interview.

You should also make a note of any particular feature or behaviour to help you consider the meaning of the body language displayed. Rather than rely on memory, you should fix the exact point in the interview when the candidate said or did something noteworthy and record what he or she did to make the statement or action remarkable. This will help you to see the body language in context and thereby avoid giving the action greater importance than it actually deserves.

Some organizations provide pro-forma interview record forms which list the criteria and provide space for notes. These can be of great assistance and help the interviewers to focus on important matters when considering which of the candidates best meets the requirements of the person specification and job.

Part 2

The questions

How to use the questions

The questions suggested in the following chapters are readymade, but how they are used is up to you, the interviewer. Used in the wrong way, at the wrong time, or asked of the wrong candidate, they may be useless or even harmful. However, used as tools, designed to elicit evidence from the candidate, they can make a positive contribution to making the best decision.

The chapters that follow cover the areas below:

- overall objectives;
- sample questions;
- typical replies;
- possible interpretations;
- probes and supplementaries.

Overall objectives

These suggest the main aims of each phase of the interview. While you should never exclude relevant information whenever you can get it, you must have a structure to what you are trying to do: the framework into which you will fit your questions.

Sample questions

It is obviously impossible to list questions that are suitable for all interviews. Some of those listed can be used as they stand in a wide range of situations, others will work well when adapted; yet others may suggest questions in the same general area that will help you gather the information you need.

To avoid repetition, questions throughout are set in **bold type**. Main questions are numbered; S indicates supplementaries.

Typical replies

It is even less possible to anticipate all the replies you may receive. However, those offered are typical of real life, and have been chosen as far as possible to illustrate the kind of attitudes and approaches that candidates are likely to take when faced with the question.

It will become clear in most cases which sort of response a candidate is making. However, you must be careful not to stereotype candidates, but to listen carefully to exactly what they say each time.

To avoid repeating the heading, typical replies are set in *italic type*.

Possible interpretations

The emphasis must be on the word 'possible'. The real meaning of any reply can only be found by fitting it in with all the other evidence you have; what the candidates have written, their other replies, body language and presentation, references, reports, test results. The interpretations suggested can, at best, do no more than help interviewers think about how they will assess each of the unique individuals who attend for interview.

The heading is usually dispensed with, and the interpretation follows the *typical reply*.

Probes and supplementaries

In many cases, the possible interpretations are followed by suggestions for probes or supplementary questions.

In the more important areas, further typical replies and their possible interpretations are offered; in others, the continuation is left open.

A suggested method of working

To get the best value from this section, you may wish to conduct a practice interview:

1. General preparation

Gather together the essential information about a job in your organization. This should include the job description, person specification and possibly an advertisement. If these documents do not exist, follow the guidance given in the first two chapters and prepare them for yourself. You can then use the documents as you read the following pages to draft questions as if you were really going to interview for that job.

2. Preparation for actual interviews

Before starting an actual interview, reread any chapters you feel might be particularly relevant to you and the job.

Draw up a simple outline plan of the way you would like the interview to go and the areas you wish to explore. Pick out questions, including supplementaries, that are related to the job description and person specification, but be sure to adapt the wording carefully to your situation, and decide approximately when during the interview you might use them. Read the likely replies and possible interpretations.

Remember, the replies are only samples of the infinite number you may get when you actually use them; it is essential that you listen carefully to what the candidate says. Remember also that the interpretations are only suggestions. See how far you agree with them, and note where you disagree.

3. During the interview

Ask a colleague to help you by acting as a candidate for the job and going through a role play interview.

Throughout the interview be ready to adapt your plan depending on what you hear. Do not use questions that have clearly become redundant or unsuitable. Using what you have learnt from the book and the approach it follows, add extra questions or supplementaries in what seems the best place. This will ensure that you gather all the information you need to assess the candidate's suitability for the job in a way that is thorough, fair and rigorous.

4. Afterwards

Check your notes against the person specification, reinterpreting the replies to make a coherent picture of the candidate. You may find it useful to work with your colleague and compare how your interpretations concur with or differ from their understanding, and consider how and why your differing views were formed.

5. Building experience

Annotate the book with your own comments and additional questions you may have used successfully, to help you next time.

However, never allow yourself to become rigid or to stereotype candidates; approach each one with an open and flexible mind, and improvise and adapt your questions, building on your own accumulating experience as well as the suggestions in this book.

four

The **welcome**

Overall objectives

1. Welcome and introductions.
2. Establishing rapport.
3. Explaining the selection process.
4. Checking what the candidate knows about the organization.
5. Checking what the candidate knows about the post to be filled.
6. Ensuring that the candidate is happy for the interview to proceed.
7. Building a smooth bridge to the rest of the interview.

The interviewer will do more talking during the opening than in later phases.

Welcome and introductions

The best place to meet the candidates is in the waiting room; this is friendlier than asking for them to be brought in. The person chairing the interview panel should meet the candidate, guide him or her to a seat, and then introduce the rest of the panel. In this way the building of rapport and a friendly atmosphere will have begun before the interview starts.

Conventional questions about the journey (provided it was not merely from the next street) may be an appropriate and gentle way into the main body of the interview.

The way interviewers view the welcome stage is of paramount importance for the success of the interview. As discussed earlier, inexperienced interviewers may make their mind up about the suitability of a candidate within the first minutes of an interview, and spend the remainder of the time seeking evidence to justify their belief. Some claim they can assess candidates from the way they walk into the room, or shake hands. But if the aim is to make the best selection, judgement must be postponed until evidence has been gathered.

Introductions should be informal, but should include the name and job title of all interviewers. If the panel is large, it can be helpful to provide a name-plate in front of each member.

The introductions also provide an opportunity to make clear the degree of formality expected by using (or not using) first names.

Introductory remarks

- ☐ Hello, my name is Malcolm Peel, I'm the Personnel Manager; I expect you remember getting a letter from me. This is Helen Green, our Chief Executive, and John Brown, the Computer Manager. Do you mind if we call you Fred?
- ☐ Good morning Mr Smith. My name is Peel, Personnel Manager. May I introduce Mrs Green, Chief Executive, and Mr Brown, Computer Manager. Please sit down.
- ☐ I think you know everyone?

Establishing rapport

The degree of rapport established can have a big effect on the success of the interview and will affect how quickly its objectives are achieved. Tense and nervous candidates will require more time than confident candidates or those already known to the interviewers.

An effective way of starting to build rapport is to open with a question that is easy for the candidate to answer. Trick questions and traps are likely to be counter-productive, and should not be used. The interpretation of the replies at this stage will concentrate on deciding whether the candidate is sufficiently at ease to move to more important matters, although information may sometimes be picked up unexpectedly. If you *do* get an apparently important response, you should judge whether to probe it at once or later; usually it is wiser to wait until later.

The opening stages should not be prolonged artificially, as to do so can increase the tension. But when you do move on, you must be conscious of the need to get on to the right wavelength before approaching difficult areas or asking probing questions.

1. How was your journey?

R1. *No problems. Your map was a great help.*
R2. *The traffic was dreadful. I was stuck behind one of these juggernauts most of the way, and there was a red car that kept on trying to overtake on bends. In the end, it nearly had me into a ditch. . .*

Replies will usually be conventional and uninformative, as with R1.

Occasionally they may suggest that the candidate is either unduly tense about travel or does not travel much. This will normally only matter if the job involves much travelling, or if the question of daily commuting would arise if the candidate were appointed. In this case the topic will need probing at some stage:

S. How long did it take you?

R1. *Not as long as I thought it might. The train only took 35 minutes, and it was an hour and a quarter door-to-door. I reckon it would just about give me time to finish the crossword.*

If the candidate comments on the question of regular travelling, it suggests that this has been considered by them. If not, it may need to be followed up later.

2. Did you receive the company's annual report?

R1. *Yes thank you. I have a number of questions to ask you about your expansion plans.*

This indicates that the candidate has prepared him- or herself. You can deal with the candidate's questions before the end of the interview.

---

* The examples of replies to questions are numbered R1, R2, R3, etc. Any supplementary questions are signified by the letter S.

3. **Are you comfortable in that chair? Can you see and hear everyone clearly?**

R1. *No, the light casts a shadow over Mrs Green's face. May I move the chair to the left?*

This allows you to demonstrate concern for the candidate and gives him or her the opportunity of making an adjustment before the main body of the interview is begun.

Explaining the selection process

You should briefly explain the process you are using and how the present interview fits into it. You should also outline how the interview is to be structured, what will be covered, in what order, and approximately how long it should last.

This will help you to exercise control as the interview progresses. If the candidate should move outside the defined area, or spend too long on a particular point, you can refer to this introductory statement, and bring the proceedings back on track.

4. **This is a preliminary interview, after which a final interview will be conducted by the whole Board, probably at the start of next month. I expect we'll want to spend about an hour together this morning. I'll tell you something about us first, and the post we want to fill. Then, I'd like to learn about you. Finally, I expect you will have some questions to ask us. Is that OK?**

R1. *Yes, fine.*
R2. *Oh, I see. As a matter of fact, I've had a final interview for another job, and they said they'd let me know by Friday. Would there be any chance of speeding things up, or at least letting me know by Friday whether you want to take this one further?*

R1 calls for no comment.

R2 might suggest that the candidate is more interested in the other job, although this is by no means certain. It is usually best to probe such a situation at once:

S.   **That could be difficult. Would you mind telling me about the other job?**

R1. *Not at all. It's with XYZ & Co. . .*
R2. *If you don't mind, I'd prefer not to go into detail.*

Having raised the issue, most candidates will talk reasonably frankly about the other job. If they do, much may be learnt, especially from its similarities to or differences from the current post, which should be probed if necessary.

R2 is difficult to interpret as it stands. This reaction may arise from general secrecy, fear of contact between the two employers, or perhaps because the application is to a trade rival.

In either case, the best hope of probing is probably to refer to the 'other job' towards the end of the interview, when it will be clearer whether a second interview is likely and the candidate will be better able to decide whether to remain under consideration. Occasionally, the 'other job' may have been forgotten by then.

If you wish to probe further now, you may try:

S.   **If they do make an offer, how will you react?** or
S.   **I doubt if our Board could get together any earlier. Would you be prepared to wait for their decision, or would you have to finalize the other offer immediately?**

R1. *That's no problem.*
R2. *I promised to let them know straight away.*

In most cases, the reply will indicate reasonable flexibility, as with R1.

R2 is an attempt to pressurize you, and suggests a strong and confident candidate. If these characteristics are on the person specification, you may be keen to continue, and work around the difficulty later.

If not, you may decide that the implied deadline can only be resisted. If the candidate is prepared to keep to your reasonable timescale, fine; if not, you can do nothing and are entitled to ask whether there is any point in continuing with the application.

Knowledge of the organization

It is useful to check the amount of knowledge the candidate has of the job and the organization. Has any effort been made to find out anything more than the information provided in the advertisement and any paperwork you sent? Have any additional sources of information (such as directories or the Internet) been consulted? If any important gaps are revealed, it will usually be necessary to repair them at once, so that the proceedings can start from the proper baseline.

Some recruiters use this as the first area of serious evaluation, on the basis that a worthwhile and serious candidate will not only have read and digested the job advertisement and any information sent out, but will have researched the organization from other sources.

5. **What do you know about Green & Co (= you)?**

R1. *Only what it said in the ad. To tell the truth, I'd never heard of you before.*

R2. *Well, I know you make medical products, have sites here and in Harlow, employ about 1500 people, and are owned by a US parent. Not much more, I'm afraid.*

R3. *I looked you up in a couple of directories, and I discovered that. . . (A detailed summary, from which the interviewers may learn a thing or two.)*

Good candidates should always have tried to research the organization to which they are applying. You may find that you are easily impressed by sound knowledge of your own operation, and upset by lack of it, especially if you are the proprietor or a senior executive. You must keep a sense of perspective, and judge the reply according to the circumstances and the seniority of the post. Be wary of flattery.

If the candidate lives in the same town or neighbourhood as the organization, a poor answer such as R1 suggests someone lacking in real interest not only in your organization, but in the world of work in general; it may be a serious deficiency.

If the candidates are making a number of applications to different organizations, for example following graduation, an efficient answer is an important indication of good faith in this specific application, and demonstrates that the candidate's thinking has got further than 'It's Tuesday, so this must be Green's.'

If the post is senior, a comprehensive answer such as R3 suggests a keen candidate, a serious application and an ability to research relevant data.

If the post is very senior (director or partner level), anything less than R3 must be seen as a grave failing.

Whatever view you take, it is necessary to fill the important gaps in the candidate's knowledge, but without overloading, for little of what is said at this stage of an interview will be remembered.

Knowledge of the post to be filled

Questioning in this area is essential, so that you can examine the candidates' understanding of the job they have applied for, fill in any important gaps, and observe their reactions to the new knowledge.

Before reaching this stage, the candidates should have read the advertisement, and any more detailed information sent or given to them while waiting for the interview. They may have been given a tour round the work area and introduced to potential colleagues.

If any of the candidates show that they have not made proper use of the information, you may be justified in questioning whether they are interested in the job. You will certainly wish to probe, and if you are dissatisfied, you may even query whether the application is worth pursuing.

On the other hand, failure to understand the nature of the post may be the result of poor or misleading information from you. In this case, you will need to tread carefully, to supply the missing detail, and to enquire whether that changes the candidate's view of the post.

As with information about the organization, there is no point in overloading the candidates, as it is unlikely they will be able to take in a mass of detail. This is a real danger if you are responsible for the area of work and enjoy talking about it to interested others.

This aspect of the selection *must* be two-way. The more accurately the candidate understands what is required, the better both parties are able to work together towards a correct decision.

The interview can be seen as a time during which information is given and collected by both parties so they are able to decide whether they want to enter into a relationship with each other. If this exchange is done in an honest and open fashion and if the information given is of the right quantity and quality (ie fit for the purpose), the chance of making the right decision is increased.

If you are using the services of a recruitment consultant, you will need to ensure that their briefing has provided sufficient information about the job and your organization so that any questions the candidates are likely to pose can be answered.

This stage can form a natural bridge from the introduction to the subsequent phases of the interview.

6. What do you know about this job?

R1. *Well, nothing except the title and the salary; I hoped you would tell me.*

R2. *Only the details you sent me. As I understand it, it's based here, although there will be travel within the UK. I will be in charge of a section of five systems analysts. The work will be for a major client, and involve a fully integrated purchase and stock control system. You require recent XYZ experience.*

R3. *I understand the title and the description you gave in the advertisement. But to be truthful, I found some aspects a little vague. My contacts tell me you are completing a big reorganization of this area, so I imagine that is why. I'm sure you will fill in the detail for me.*

R1 is weak. Unless there is some special factor (like an internal candidate who was instructed to apply for a newly created post) you may want to probe at once:

S. **Then why did you apply?**

R2 is a sensible, standard reply, but you may want to add a few additional details.

R3 places the ball firmly in your court. It appears to be the reply of a potentially appointable candidate who deserves an explanation if the remarks are justified. Over to you.

When you have answered the candidates' questions, you would be wise to check:

S. **Does all that make sense, or are there any other aspects you would like to clear up before we go on?**

The reply to this may reveal the need for further information, or to correct misunderstanding. At worst, it may lead to a mutual parting of the ways.

Is all well?

By this stage, you will have prepared the ground, and be ready to move into the more testing phases of the interview. You should have established a reasonably easy relationship with the candidate, who should be talking in a more relaxed and open fashion. You will have established what is known about your organization and the job applied for, and filled in any gaps. You may also have gathered some information about why the candidate is interested in the job. If there are any doubts, there is a reasonable chance you may already have brought them to the surface.

However, very occasionally, an interview may collapse at this point; either you or the candidate may discover that you have a fundamental misunderstanding about the job, and realize that the most sensible course is to face this and halt the proceedings without further waste of time.

Something may have weakened the candidate's interest in going further. You may doubt whether the candidate is really interested or understands what the job is about. This may have been suggested by a strange answer or by the candidate's appearing to be either unduly anxious or excessively confident. If you have any reason to be unsure, you may be advised to find out now, and not go blindly into the next phase.

---

7. Is this what you expected when you applied, or have there been any surprises in what you have learnt?

R1. *No, that's fine, thanks. Just what I had expected from the advertisement.*

R2. *I think so . . . I wasn't completely clear whether you are prepared to appoint above the minimum of the salary range.*

R3. *Yes. I wasn't sure from what you said whether I would report to the marketing director or the sales manager. I already report to a director, and I wouldn't want to take a step down.*

R4. *Could you enlarge on what you said about the travelling? We have two young children, and I don't want to spend many nights away from home, at the present time.*

The candidate may be too embarrassed to admit to serious problems, and may mention them, if at all, only indirectly. You are looking for something that sounds firm and convincing, like R1. Hesitation or double-takes in the answer may thus be significant. R2, R3 and R4 all suggest possible difficulties and cannot be passed over without probing. For R2, you may probe:

S. **We hardly ever do that. Let me see; you're on 20k at the moment. We would start whoever we appointed on 20, which is the bottom of the range, as you know. Would this be acceptable to you? If not, what are you looking for?**

R1. *Well, I thought from the ad that you would pay anything within the range if you found the right candidate. Of course, the job's exactly what I'm after, but I'd have to travel further, and I don't want to take a drop.*

This sounds very negative. Such a candidate may pull out at some stage if money is that critical, so why waste each other's time? If you really can't pay above the minimum and the candidate is not prepared to accept less for a job he or she really wants, the right course would probably be to face facts and terminate the interview now.

R3 and R4 need similar probes:

S.   **No, you would report to the sales manager. I wouldn't want there to be any doubt about that.**

S.   **It would vary, of course; some weeks would be spent entirely in the office; occasionally, you might be away the whole week if, say, you were visiting our agents in Scotland. But the person who took this post would have to be prepared to average about two nights away each week.**

In each case, anything less than a convincing, credible acceptance of the position suggests both parties should bite the bullet and terminate the interview now:

S.   **It seems as though the job is not what you were expecting. In view of what you say, I think the wisest course is for us to face facts now, rather than waste any more of each other's time, and admit that this post is not for you. Do you agree?**

Building a smooth bridge

It is a common mistake to conclude the introductory phase with a pause, a change of tone, and something which sounds like (or even says in so many words) 'Right, we've played around long enough, now let's get down to business.' If you do this, you risk spoiling all you have done to relax the candidate, establish rapport, and get him or her talking freely.

The next phase will be an examination of the candidate's employment history and other relevant information about his or her background. The CV or application form will give you some facts to use for your opening questions. The smoothest bridge is often to pick some relatively neutral aspect and ask a broad, not unduly demanding question. By using this, you can also begin to learn something of the candidate's interests and expectations.

However, there are also traps for the interviewer in the use of this sort of question, and you must beware.

The Human Rights Act 1998 gives a person the right to respect for private and family life. Your questions should therefore be designed and used to give useful information about the candidate's potential ability to do the job. You should try to avoid the temptation to seek those candidates whose background is similar to your own. If you fall into this trap you may find yourself being accused of discrimination.

8. How did you enjoy your time at school?

R1. *I had a great time. We were quite a good year, though I say it myself. All but three went on to university, and the others went straight into a job. We still meet up every year around New Year.*

R2. *It was OK, although the school was too large. The Head didn't know all the teachers, let alone pupils.*

R3. *I got good GCSEs, but I couldn't stay on to do 'A' levels. My dad was redundant by then, and mum wasn't very well.*

The importance of these replies will depend on how long ago it all was. If you are interviewing a school-leaver or a graduate, schooldays will be vastly more important than with a 40-year-old, for whom more recent events will give you the opening question.

You should avoid the temptation of making judgements about those who went to university as opposed to those who, for whatever reason, did not have the opportunity – unless, of course, a degree is required. Rather, the above responses provide other potentially useful information.

R1 suggests a candidate who likes a certain degree of stability and constancy. You know that he or she has a number of long-term friendships, which are renewed each year. You may wish to explore how the candidate will respond to changes that may disrupt routine.

R2 tells you that the candidate felt a little isolated in a large organization and may prefer to be a part of a smaller organization in which people are known to each other. If your organization is very big, it may be important to find out how the candidate will respond to being a 'small cog in a large wheel'.

R3 tells you that the candidate may have a higher level of academic potential than his or her GCSEs indicate but family circumstances prevented further achievement. You may wish to find out if the candidate has any plans for further study.

---

9. **It's interesting to meet someone else who has spent time doing voluntary work. What, looking back, do you feel you got from it?**

R1. *Not a lot. I felt I was expected to do a lot of menial work for very little thanks.*
R2. *Wonderful time. I'm certain that if we had a national system for community work, most of the problems with today's youth would disappear overnight. And it would help with drugs and crime.*
R3. *Mixed, I think. I did learn a lot about myself which I doubt I could have done without it. But a lot of the time was totally wasted.*

This can be dangerous ground. It opens up social attitudes, loyalties and other biases which may be held strongly by interviewer or interviewee.

Bad interviewers may be trapped into awarding high marks to someone whose prejudices match their own. Good interviewers will be prepared to use such information and relate it to the needs of the job and exclude their own biases and preconceptions. If it does not relate, such information should be discounted. The value of the information lies in what it tells you about the way candidates approach work and see their experiences.

R1 appears superficial, and suggests a candidate who does tasks with an expectation of some reward. You will need to watch to see whether other replies reinforce or cancel out this impression.

As far as it goes, R2 suggests someone with strong views on social issues. Whether or not you agree with them, at least it indicates that the individual is aware of what is happening in the wider world. You must avoid prejudice and watch for evidence from less highly charged subjects.

R3 appears to indicate mature and sensible analysis. However, it might suggest someone who wants to be active all the time. Further exploration of the last statement may be merited.

---

10. **Work-based experience seems to be coming back. What do you think of this change, based on your own time as a craft apprentice?**

R1. *I think it's a mistake. Five years was a long time, sure. You learnt with your hands and developed a lot of skill. But without some explanation you never knew why you were doing something.*

R2. *It all depends on who is teaching you. We have lost a lot of skills. It could just be another political gimmick.*

R3. *All these trainees are just sweated labour. The bosses just wanted an excuse to cut wages.*

Here also, there is a danger of warming to political biases that match your own – for this reason, it may be dangerous. However it can, with care, be legitimately used to assess the quality and maturity of thought.

You will need to probe each reply further, and avoid, in doing so, getting drawn into controversy or argument, especially if the jobholder is going to be involved in implementing such initiatives.

five

The **CV: times past**

Overall objectives

1. To fill factual gaps in the CV and probe any areas where the information given is incomplete.
2. To learn about past behaviour which may help to predict behaviour in the post to be filled.
3. To explore levels of competency.

Using the CV in date order provides a sequence for questioning which has a logic for both candidate and interviewer. It provides a natural order and a built-in memory jogger. It makes it easier for the candidate to explain and for the interviewer to understand the way events have unrolled and the pattern they have formed. It also provides a built-in checklist to ensure nothing of importance is forgotten.

This approach also recognizes that the best predictor of future behaviour is past behaviour, when correctly understood and interpreted. This is not to say that an individual will act in the same way next time; the action previously taken may not have worked and the person could have learnt from the experience. Nothing can predict human reactions with certainty, but the past is usually the best guide available.

When using the CV in this way, you will need to keep a sense of proportion. Some areas will be passed over quickly; there may be no need to explore O-level grades, for example, when interviewing a 40-year-old PhD. But others may be of unexpected importance; you may wish to spend a good deal of time on why a particular project failed, especially if it bears close similarity to a major element in the present job.

The use of the CV will usually form an excellent basis for the main section of the interview during which exploration of competency, knowledge, attributes and the longer-term future will be conducted.

(Needless to say, this must *not* be the first time you have studied the CV. For effective selection you should have done this at least twice before; once when making up the list for the interview, and once when preparing before the interviews themselves.)

Filling in the gaps

Any gap may suggest that something is being concealed, and filling it may reveal relevant information. You have no time to waste and must tread a path between naive trust and small-minded suspicion, but human nature being what it is, it is usually safer to err on the side of suspicion. People do tell lies to get themselves into a job.

A time gap in a CV must raise suspicions that something is being hidden. The candidate may have been:

- in a job that doesn't fit the rest of the CV;
- in a job from which he or she was dismissed;
- unemployed;
- in hospital;
- in jail;
- out of the country;
- repeating a part of a course.

The possibility of someone actually forgetting what they were doing is remote, especially as a gap will form part of a sequence of events. But before jumping to the more extreme conclusions, it is sensible to find out whether it is a simple oversight in completing the paperwork or mistake.

Whatever answer is given, it will almost certainly need probing, but in doing so you must avoid sounding inquisitorial. You may wish to remind yourself of the mistakes you may have made in your own career, and of the fact that, for example, hospital and jail are places of recovery and rehabilitation. Likewise, many people

lose their jobs due to reasons beyond their control. You are not there
to judge; you simply need to know and begin to build a relationship
built on honesty and trust.

Gap filling will go on at the same time as you are engaged on
other aspects of this phase:

1. **You don't say what you were doing between leaving
   Black's in July 1995 and joining White's in April
   1996.**

R1. *I wasn't at all sure what I wanted to do, so I tried one or two
temporary jobs.*
R2. *No, actually I was job hunting then.*
R3. *I was self-employed.*
R4. *Oh, didn't I put that in? I worked as a bus driver in Liverpool.*

R1 has a good chance of being correct, but you will need to probe:

S. **What actually were the temporary jobs, and who were they
with?** (Writing down the answers as given will concentrate
the interviewee's mind.)
S. **What went wrong?** (Of each in turn.)

R2 could mean anything. There is nothing wrong with job hunting,
particularly in times of massive unemployment, but you need to
know if departure from the previous job was forced. You may try
a succession of probes:

S. **Why did you leave your previous job, if you had nothing
lined up?**
S. **What sort of jobs were you applying for, and how many
applications did you make?**
S. **What seemed to hold you back from getting any of them?**

If the statement is true, you may acquire information of relevance
to the present application.

Probes for R3 may be:

S. **What did you hope for when you started the enterprise?**
S. **How did it go, and what went wrong in the end?**

It will be easier to be satisfied of the truth of this statement than the others, as self-employment is usually a matter of pride, even if it goes wrong. It will certainly tell a great deal about the candidate.

R4 sounds convincing, but should be probed:

S.   **That's an interesting move; why did you do that?**
S.   **What made you leave your job?**
S.   **Why, as a matter of interest, didn't you mention it in your CV?**

2.   You say you got an honours degree, but not which class.

R1. *Sorry; it was a third.*
R2. *Second class.*

R1 sets the record straight, and without too much damage.

R2 does not. The difference between the classes of degree is significant, as every graduate knows. If candidates cannot remember their grade or level of qualification, especially if recently attained, you may have just cause for suspicion. It requires the follow-up:

S.   **Upper or lower?**

The need to press this may leave a doubt as to the openness of the candidate.

3.   Why did you leave the course before its end?

R1. *Things were very busy at work and I found that I could not give the course work the attention it deserved. I would like to go back to it some time in the future.*
R2. *It was tough going.*

The first reply is plausible, as this reason for withdrawing from a course is not uncommon. The second, though, tells you nothing about the candidate or the situation. There may be several reasons why the candidate found the course hard, some of which may have nothing to do with the individual's ability or commitment. Clearly further probing is called for.

Relating past to future

To try to project the candidate's future behaviour from how he or she has behaved in the past is the centre of the interview. There is much you could ask, and you will need to choose with care.

4. Why did you decide to go into computing when you got your degree?

R1. *Most of my friends were doing the same thing. IBZ came on the milkround, and gave us very impressive interviews. The prospects looked fabulous.*

R2. *Well, a classics degree doesn't really lead anywhere directly. I looked around a bit and this was first to come up.*

R3. *I'd been interested in computing since my dad got a micro when I was about 13. I worked in XYZ in the summer vacations, the first operating on shifts, and the second on a big software project they had on.*

The reasons for a graduate's first job choice may be far less clear than might be supposed. The majority of students study a subject because they are good at it, occasionally because they prefer certain teachers. Arts subjects in particular are rarely chosen for vocational reasons.

None of these replies need be seen as unfavourable, although R3 is clearly the most convincing and suggests someone with a long-term commitment to the chosen career.

R1 and R2 will probably need follow-up:

S. **How do you feel about the choice now?**

5. What made you leave White's after 10 years with them?

R1. *They had just lost a couple of their biggest clients, and things didn't look good. There was a lot of talk of redundancies in the offing.*

R2. *I couldn't see any chances of more promotion. My boss was younger than me, and his boss had only been in a year, and looked set to stay a long while.*

R3. *Black's were advertising for people with just my background, but at 3k a year more than I was getting.*

R4. *I was made redundant.*

R5. *I had a flaming row with my boss.*

R6. *They asked me to resign.*

A change of employer in mid-career is still a cause of suspicion to some. They may feel that to leave after about a decade of service with one employer demonstrates failure. By that time a person's potential should be fully known, and if the work is no longer satisfying, no longer presents a challenge or makes poor use of the individual's talents, perhaps the person has plateaued. Other recruiters would not share this view, but most would feel that a change after such a period does merit an explanation.

R1 could be just such a reasonable explanation, but is worth a probe:

S. **What happened to the firm, in the end?**

R2 may also be perfectly valid. Careers easily become plateaued in their middle years through no fault of their owner. But a probe is justified:

S. **How did any further progress become prevented?**

R3 likewise may be fine. The probe might be:

S. **Were you able to do anything about this?**

The stigma of redundancy should have largely disappeared. Usually it is not caused by the individual. Nevertheless, R4 must be probed. 'Redundancy' may mean anything, from a well-compensated, mass reduction in employees to a polite synonym for an individual sacking. Occasionally, with longer serving employees, even the person involved may not realize the full implications of what happened to them. Follow-ups might begin:

S. **Can you tell me more about the exact circumstances of your redundancy?**

This may be followed by more detailed probes.

R5 appears to be refreshingly direct and apparently honest, but the circumstances behind the argument should be explored. R6 is a real pre-emptive strike. Both replies clearly invite follow-up, and the interviewer should dig beneath the surface:

S. **Go on; please tell me the detail.**

---

6. Tell me about your relationship with your boss during this phase.

R1. *Just ordinary. No problems.*
R2. *She was an interesting character. In many ways the best I've worked for, but in some ways she could be a little difficult.*
R3. *I found him impossible. He took all the credit, and passed on all the blame. He was one of the main reasons I left.*
R4. *A great person. Working with him was better than studying for an MBA (Master of Business Administration degree). I learnt most of what I know from him.*

Attitude towards the boss is one of the most transferable of work behaviours. It often reflects deep-seated views of authority in general, and can be rooted in childhood. If you can learn anything of the candidate's attitude to past bosses, you may learn how he or she would work with you if offered the job.

Boss-attitude can also be a good indicator of the kind of job satisfaction the candidate hopes for.

R1 is defensive and non-committal. You may try a couple of probes, to establish whether it is a deliberate response, or just a weak answer:

S. **How good was she to work for?**
S. **What problems did you find working for her?**

R2 is diplomatically phrased, but tends towards the negative. It invites follow-up, although as always the response must not automatically be taken at face value:

S. **Tell me more.**

R3 may be an honest statement of fact, or sour grapes. The candidate, being involved in the situation, may not be able to disentangle the whole truth. You must at least try:

S.   **That is very sad. Can you given me one or two instances?**

R4 sounds absolutely super, which augurs well for future bosses. However, it may be given because the candidate thinks this is what you want to hear. If this is the case, your chances of getting the honest answer are slim without more detailed probing:

S.   **Can you give me a specific example of the sort of thing he did?**

---

7. What do you feel was your most worthwhile achievement at Brown's, and why?

R1. *Well, there were a lot really. Nothing very specific, but keeping the job going was an achievement, you know.*
R2. *Oh, sorting out the Borneo assignment. The Japanese were after it. That was worth about £2m, plus follow-up business.*
R3. *There was no chance of any achievements. The job just didn't give the scope; that was why I left.*
R4. *Well-motivated and trained staff. That was my best achievement.*

Detailed answers to this question can tell a great deal about the candidate's quality of work and motivational systems.

R1 sounds vague and wishy-washy, the answer of a candidate whose interest in work may be low. You may try a probe by repeating the question in different words:

S.   **Did you do anything you were particularly proud of?**

Without more detail you will probably pass on discouraged.

R2 should be the good one, specific and testable. You can probe:

S.   **Great. Tell me about it.**

R3 is the ultimate negative. But the negative may be a reflection of the job rather than the candidate. You must try to find out which.

One of the biggest traps waiting for the unwary interviewer is called causal bias. It is often assumed that an individual is responsible for what happens to him- or herself – the cause of events. Sometimes, though, the individual may be an innocent party, simply affected by what is happening. The job of the interviewer is to ascertain exactly what role the candidate played in events:

S. **What exactly was holding you back?**

R4 sounds suspiciously like a rehearsed reply. It may be real, it may be a play for time, or it may be the only thing the candidate can think of. You must probe:

S. **Yes, of course. What, under your guidance, was your staff's finest achievement?**

---

8. What problems did you meet when they first made you a supervisor, and how did you cope with them?

R1. *Not a lot, really. It all worked out smoothly.*
R2. *I found it quite difficult, especially as they gave me no training. The worst was sorting out the lengthy tea breaks everyone took. It took weeks to re-establish the rules. In the end I had to discipline one man, right through the procedure to final warning, before he came round.*
R3. *Budgeting was a bit of a headache. It wasn't just me; no one seemed to understand it.*

People are naturally loath to admit to difficulties at interview, even when invited to say how they overcame them.

R1 is evasive and sounds unlikely or the response of a candidate with limited experience. Probing might help something to the surface, but probably won't.

R2 sounds specific and frank, and gives an indication of a genuine problem faced and solved.

R3 is weak as it stands, suggesting a general problem. You will need to probe further to find out more about the candidate's own difficulties:

S.   **What problems did it cause you?**

The reply to this may need further detailed probing.

---

9.   Why did you take the post at Yellowlease College?

R1. *It was what I had always wanted. I felt there was a really worthwhile job to be done with those young people, and I knew by then I had got the experience to help them.*

R2. *It was an opportunity to broaden my experience. This was a job at the right level, and it paid very well.*

R3. *I'd exhausted what Brown's had to offer, and I was ready to move on.*

The reasons for previous job moves should be informative, suggesting the sort of approach the candidate may be taking to the present application. Somehow this rarely works out so clearly at interview. If there is a good rise in salary or better prospects, the candidate will probably feel the reasons are self-evident, although he or she will rarely say so in so many words. Often a probe produces more information than the original question.

R1 sounds positive and clear. The motivation is specific and forward looking and is plausible, combining interest in the job with interest in people. You can follow up:

S.   **How did it work out once you got there?**

R2 is a little vague, and needs to be supplemented by more information about the opportunities.

R3 looks backwards, not even mentioning the new job or employer. A probe for both this and R2 might be:

S.   **What are your feelings about the move, looking back from where you are now?**

---

10.   Looking back on your career so far, how do you feel about the way it has worked out?

R1. *It's strange how things happen. When I started, I intended to make a career in retailing, but the opportunities were never there. I've given* up trying to plan the future now. I don't think it's worked out too badly, despite the changes.

R2. *Not as well as I'd hoped, but then youth always is impatient. I wasted two good years at Brown's. Then came the recession of the early nineties. But I've got back on the road since then.*

R3. *I qualified as a chemist, and chemistry was what I wanted to do. But in those days I didn't realise how limited the opportunities for specialists are. I was hesitant about moving into management, but now I've done it, I know I've found my feet. Looking back, compared with management, chemistry was narrow and dull.*

R4. *Bang on target. When I left school, I promised myself I would take five years to look around, five years to build a base, and then go for it. That's just what I've done, and now I'm ready to start motoring.*

This question only makes sense with candidates who have been around for a few years, but with such people it can tell a lot. They may not have thought this way before, and replies may be surprisingly frank.

R1 is rather sad. The individual has experienced some disappointment. You will have to probe to find out whether the individual was a victim of circumstances or was not able to control his or her own destiny.

R2 sounds a sensible appraisal. Its failing is its lack of reference to the work itself; 'on the road' in itself is meaningless.

R3 inspires a lot of confidence. It is specific, well expressed and covers both work content and personal growth. By implication it looks forward to the next move.

R4 gives the impression of a rehearsed answer. The best that can be said is that it is crisp and confident, and that the individual may have thought about possible questions before the interview.

---

11. What has been the most satisfying achievement in your career to date?

R1. *Keeping my first boss happy. He was someone no one else could get on with.*

R2. *It was when I was in the labs, and suddenly I came up with an answer to the corrosion problem our main model was experiencing in tropical conditions. Almost by chance.*

R3. *Landing the Scandinavian contract. It was worth over £1m, and it had taken me nine months and eight visits to Stockholm to bring to a close.*

R1 may or may not suggest a candidate with remarkable inter-personal skills, but you cannot be sure from the way the reply is phrased. You must probe:

S. **How did you do that?**

R2 may be spoilt by the 'chance' aspect, but much may depend on how readily others accepted the discovery and whether the cand-idate was solely responsible for the find. You should follow up:

S. **How did the engineers take your discovery?**

R3 seems to suggest a candidate who can identify a clear target and put in much hard work before the goal is attained. A simple request for more detail may be worthwhile.

---

12. Tell me about the worst disagreement you have experienced during your career, and what came of it.

R1. *I don't think I can remember any bad ones.*
R2. *I had a problem with one of the district reps once on the phone. She couldn't understand, or made out she couldn't, what I was telling her. In the end I slammed the phone down on her. She told her boss, who told mine, who reprimanded me. I still feel a bit sore about it, but I expect I was in the wrong really.*
R3. *There was a chap in the drawing office, and for some reason we could not work together. No idea why – body chemistry or something. The trouble was, as members of the same team, we saw each other every day. I tried all I knew, short of shooting the guy, but he didn't want to know. Then one day I happened to walk into the office carrying a copy of a gardening magazine. That did it; he's been my closest pal at the place for a couple of years now.*

R1 is another conversation stopper; there seems little point in attempting a probe or supplementary question.

R2 and R3 both suggest reasonable insight into the candidate's relationships, and apparent honesty. On balance, R3 seems to be the story of someone with nothing to hide, and the incident sounds like a one-off, while R2 just might be the tip of an iceberg, possibly even a muted call for help.

Professional and technical competence

Surprisingly, competence can be a problem in selection. You need to be specific about the level of professional or technical expertise, but, while this may be outlined in the person specification, assessing its possession is not easy. Several things may go wrong.

Different perspectives

Competence may be emphasized too much, on the assumption that an 'expert' has everything, or nearly everything, that matters for the performance of the job. On the other hand, it may be played down too much, in the belief that the necessary expertise can be learnt, but the required approach cannot. These differing perspectives may become a point of conflict between the interviewers if they have not prepared themselves adequately and considered the importance of all factors in the person specification.

Failure to assess

Competence may remain unassessed, even by those who are convinced that it matters.

It is easy to assume that the possession of a suitable qualification or previous experience are adequate evidence of competence. It may also be felt that there is no meaningful way it can be assessed during an interview. Some interviewers may be wary of trying to assess specific knowledge or expertise. Even those with similar knowledge may be hesitant, fearing perhaps that they may be out of date, that an interviewee may know more than they do, or even that it is 'not the done thing' to doubt or question a fellow professional's knowledge.

Occasionally, exploring competence may fall between different interviewers, everyone assuming that the others have assessed or will assess it.

The need to assess

The need to assess competence will depend on what the person specification requires, but there are few jobs in which it does not figure. However, the interview may not always be the only vehicle for assessment; performance tests, work samples and references have a part to play.

The non-expert

Although the basic principles are the same, the type of questions intended to explore professional or technical expertise are outside the scope of this book, as they will be specific to each area.

Laypeople cannot legitimately test knowledge and skills. If you tried to do so, using only superficial knowledge, it might suggest to the candidate that you do not know the subject area. This could lay you open to the danger of being 'blinded by science'. Most importantly, you would not have the means of evaluating what was said.

However, a non-expert can legitimately attempt to build up a picture of how the candidates assess their own skills, how they have used them and where development needs lie, all of which is useful.

If detailed assessment of competence is needed, you should use an 'expert' who has sufficient expertise.

---

13. **What have you done since you first qualified to keep your knowledge up to date?**

R1. *Little outside my job. But I find that everyday experience is a very effective way of learning.*

R2. *That was rather a long time ago, of course. I read quite a bit: journals, papers and so on. White's sent me on a couple of courses last year.*

R3. *I choose a course of some sort every year. This year I've started with the Open University, although to be honest I'm finding it a bit of a struggle so far.*

Attitudes towards skill updating vary enormously, as do individual circumstances and opportunities.

This is an area of great importance. Skills and, especially, professional and technical knowledge do become out of date. Accepting this and being prepared to act on developmental needs is now seen as a critical competency. If we are keen on education, training and obtaining qualifications for ourselves and those who work with us, we may be too insistent with those having different views. The operative factors are ambition, age, and the rate of technical obsolescence in the relevant area.

R1 is very relaxed, and inappropriate either for a person new to the area of work or someone in a rapidly changing environment. It is hardly an inspiring reply.

R2 suggests that the candidate may be a little relaxed about the need to keep up to date. The attitude should be probed, however:

S.   **Do you feel there is a danger of personal obsolescence? Might you be missing out?**

R3 sounds great. You will, however, need to find out what the 'courses' were, what subjects are being studied through the Open University, and the reasons for the difficulties.

_____

14. What are the three most important skills that you have developed in your career so far?

R1. *Number one is easy; keeping the working relationship good both without and in the team. Number two; well, I suppose the skill of prioritizing work. As for number three; I think I've developed a nose for the oddball, to mix metaphors; an instinct for something out of place – something that might go badly wrong (or sometimes right).*

R2. *Problem-solving, getting information out of other people, and making sure I've done my homework.*

R3. *I've learnt that people matter more than facts, and a bit about how to handle them. I think I communicate well with almost everyone I work with, whatever level. I'm sure I have learnt how to sift out the irrelevant and remember the facts that really matter.*

R4. *I have become thoroughly computer-literate. I've learnt how to sell ideas, and I think I can weigh up people.*

The typical answers to this kind of question tend to home in on the 'soft' areas such as people skills, rather than the 'hard' areas of work skill. R4 mentions computer-literacy, and suggests a slightly different approach to the others.

These sorts of replies can be useful, as many of the items listed can be made the subject of a probe that will enter the area of job skills in some depth:

S. **Your answer suggests there was a possibility of conflict. Tell me how you go about keeping relationships good.**
S. **Tell me of one or two problems you have faced and how you solved them.**
S. **What sort of facts do really matter in your present job?**
S. **How do you use your computer skills in what you do now?**

---

15. **White's have quite a reputation in this kind of work. From your time with them, what, without giving away secrets, do they do better than the rest of us?**

R1. *They certainly set very high standards. Everyone gets at least a week's training before they are allowed to touch an assignment, and we have regular team training half-days every month.*

R2. *I'm not sure there's anything really. It's difficult to judge from inside.*

R3. *They probably have more people on the job than other firms. We have six in our section, with only 100 clients between us.*

R4. *I think they are better than many, if I can say that without offence. Their systems were set up originally by Mr White himself, but every two years a consultant updates them. They're all set out in a magnificent manual, which we all use. I guess I'd better not say much more, though.*

R2 suggests that the candidate is not very aware.

Both R1 and R4 sound meaty; R1 is open to probing, which should reveal useful information about the nature and level of the candidate's skills:

S. **What subjects would be covered in a typical training session?**

R4 has, accepting the invitation, carefully shut out the possibility of a probe, and you must leave it there.

R3 is wide open to detailed probing and comparison. This may reveal an organization with a large number of staff. It may suggest that it is very inefficient, that its staff are not very competent or that it is very committed to high standards of customer care. You will need to find out which:

S. **We have five for about 100 clients. But our section is responsible from first enquiry to debt collection. Which stages do your people cover?** (And so on.)

six

The **present: the job**

Overall objectives

1. To explore the scope and responsibilities of the candidate's present or most recent post or any work-relevant experience.
2. To match what the candidate has to offer with the needs of the post to be filled.
3. To explore expectations in regard to pay, conditions and opportunities.

This phase consists of bringing up to date the exploration of the CV which was started in the previous phase, and relating it to the current vacancy.

The scope and responsibilities of the candidate's present or most recent post

Few people, especially in professional and more senior positions, move at random from one area or kind of work to another. Therefore, unless something has gone badly wrong, there will be a close relationship between the job the candidates are now doing and the job they may reasonably hope to do next. Some people do make step changes, or revert successfully to a previous phase of their career. But even in such cases, the present job will be of great importance, if only to indicate what is being left and why.

The candidates' assessment of satisfactions and successes, failures and problems in their present job will show much about their skills and approach.

_____

1. Tell me what your responsibilities are in your present job.

R1. *Well, I'm called administration officer. I do the paperwork for all the meetings, and report to the directors each month on how things are going.*

R2. *I have four main tasks; to service the management committee, and act as the point of liaison between it and the rest of the organization; to manage the MD's private office; to control the strategic planning section; and to organize the annual conference. A mixed bag certainly, but full of fun.*

R3. *My main job is to make sure that the managing director knows what's going on, and to keep people sweet. I'm the MD's eyes and ears, especially as far as the senior management is concerned.*

R4. *I spend most of my time trying to see into the future. We like to think we have some of the best long-range planners in the country. I also pull in a number of bits and pieces no one else wants, like the annual conference.*

The way someone describes the responsibilities of the present post may be an indicator of how he or she approaches it and how success is judged. The aspects emphasized, those not mentioned, and the general shape and clarity of the reply can tell you a good deal.

However, there are two important caveats. First, the more articulate candidate will explain better than the less articulate, and you must remember how prominently this skill figures in the person specification; you may not be looking for this. Second, this is an easy question to foresee and plan for. The probes may reveal more than the original question.

R1 sounds low level for what must be seen as a responsible post. Unless the candidate is still unduly nervous, or there are other special reasons, you may well question the complexity of the work and degree of involvement.

R2, on the other hand, is particularly crisp and well balanced. If supported by other evidence, it suggests someone with a good grasp of the job.

R3 and R4 offer very different views of the same post. R3 emphasizes the communication and human relationship aspects, while R4 concentrates on the sophistication of the long-range planning job to the open dismissal of the other responsibilities. The likelihood in both cases must be that the neglected areas are outside the candidates' interests and probably skills.

---

2. Can you explain to me how your present post fits into the structure of your organization?

R1. *I work for the personnel director. I organize the management training courses for the division and keep our instructors up to date.*

R2. *I report to the site director, although I also have a functional line to the company training manager. I have a staff of eleven; five instructors, two office staff, my secretary, one technician and two cleaners.*

R3. *I'm responsible for all management development activities within the division, answerable to the managing director.*

Many candidates feel an understandable need to exaggerate their importance within their organization. The commonest way of doing this is to blur reporting lines, perhaps by forgetting layers above them, or making the indirect responsibilities of colleagues sound like a boss/subordinate relationship.

R1 sounds as if it is doing this. You will certainly need to probe:

S. **Could you sketch the structure within your area, please, to show me just how everyone relates?**

R2 appears precise and understandable, and if it is consistent with other information, you cannot ask for more.

R3 is not detailed and may suggest deliberate evasion. You may need to probe.

---

3. How is your effectiveness in your present post measured?

R1. *Well, er, we all have budgets and things. I suppose the best indication is lack of complaints. People soon complain if things go wrong.*

R2. *It's measured at annual appraisal. We have objectives which are recorded and reviewed each year. The objectives relate to the business plan and apart from information on meeting targets feedback from my boss and my colleagues is the best measure I have.*

R3. *The principal measure is the budget. I have both a cost and a revenue budget, for which I am fully accountable. The bottom line is what counts most. Apart from this, I have a great deal of freedom to make my own mistakes.*

R4. *I like to set myself the highest standards. I monitor our delivery performance weekly, and also the monthly sales of every item. I record every complaint, and personally check the cause and the action taken.*

Failure to answer this question impressively must not always be laid at the door of the candidate. In many cases, a poor answer may also be a truthful one, and the fault of the candidate's boss or the organization.

However, few effective employees will sound happy if their work is inadequately evaluated, and the reaction of the candidate to the situation is often more significant than the situation itself.

R1 sounds as if the candidate hasn't even thought about the subject before.

R2 gives the impression of someone working within a clear framework and aware of his or her context.

R3 is crisp and clear but limited only to financial measures. You will need to probe:

S. **How often do you meet your boss, and what do you discuss when you meet?**

R4 appears very positive; someone who feels the need to monitor their own work closely, probably in the absence of effective external control. You will probably want to probe this:

S. **How do your boss and the organization monitor your success?**

4. Tell me of a recent project, explaining what aspects gave you most satisfaction.

R1. *That's the snag with my present job. It gives me hardly any scope to make my own decisions.*

R2. *They asked me to reorganize the export documentation. I read up on benchmarking, and visited four other firms, including, would you believe, our main competitor. I identified 15 ways we could improve it, which saved over £150,000 a year, and made it over two days quicker. My boss said the report was the best she had seen for years, and gave a copy of it to her director.*

R3. *I changed the way we purchase office supplies. It took me nearly a year. I fell foul of the office services manager, and it turned out later that the previous supplier was a golfing friend of the MD. But I got it through in the end, and saved nearly £20,000.*

It is not enough to plan carefully, to achieve good interpersonal relations or effective communications. The ultimate test of success is to achieve the goal.

R1 is sad. There are many jobs without enough scope, but few in which someone with drive cannot achieve at least some satisfaction.

Depending on the view other answers have given of the candidate, you may feel a supplementary question is worthwhile:

S. What decisions would you like to have taken?

R2 clearly describes an interesting assignment, which probably demonstrates a number of valuable skills. But there is a notable lack of reference to implementation of the proposed change, and your assessment of the candidate will probably depend on the answer to a probe such as:

S. How many of your recommendations have actually been implemented?

R3 sounds good; an honest description of difficulties overcome. But in case of 'flannel', a probe will make the situation even clearer:

S. How did you manage it?

5. **What problems have you met in relationships with your present colleagues, and what techniques have you developed to overcome them?**

R1. *None, really. We're on very good terms.*

R2. *I suppose the biggest problems were with the warehouse people. They're not the highest calibre of staff down there, and communication can be a problem. In the end, I've found writing memos the best way of helping them remember.*

R3. *Maybe I shouldn't say it, but I found problems getting on the best terms with some of the sales staff. They're a race I don't understand very well, and they certainly don't seem to understand me. I haven't altogether cracked the problem yet, but I think I'm making progress slowly.*

You are likely to get no more from trying to probe R1 than you already have. But you may need to probe a little to make sure that this is not an evasive reply.

R2 gives the clear impression of a person prepared to help colleagues. But you can still probe:

S. **That is commendable. How do you make sure everyone stays on good terms?**

R3 is worrying and merits more detailed exploration. While one difficulty is admitted, the general impression created is that other relationships are good. So follow up with:

S. **What do you think is the cause of the problem and what action are you taking?**

---

6. **Why do you want to leave your present post?**

R1. *Well, I find the work boring now, and of course Black's don't pay well. . .*

R2. *Career progression. I've been at Black's for three years now, and the time has come to make a move.*

R3. *In many ways I'm very happy where I am; I'm not looking around actively. But the post you are filling seems to me the chance of a lifetime; it calls for the skills I have and offers the scope I want.*

R4. *My boss and I have fallen out. Life has been tough for a while, but now it's become impossible.*

This is as near a compulsory question as any on the list, but for that reason it is easy to anticipate and prepare for, and may tell you little. To be of value, the replies will need comparison with your other data. You may decide that question 7 offers a greater chance of drawing out more useful information.

R1 is weak and negative. The most charitable interpretation must be that the candidate has prepared badly.

R2 is not a lot better; it says nothing positive, and may hide negative reasons.

R3 sounds like an honest reply. It denies problems in the present post, while emphasizing the closeness of fit with the post you are filling. However, to be convincing, what it says must match up with the other data you have.

R4 appears startlingly frank, and may be the reply of an honest candidate. On the other hand, it may be a pre-emptive strike designed to defend a dodgy problem, such as just having been fired, or someone reluctant to accept authority. To find out which, you must probe now, and compare with your other data. An open question is called for:

S.   **Please tell me more.**

The match with what the candidate has to offer

You will already have started to form an opinion about this, based on the examination of the CV, and what it has shown about the candidate's experience, knowledge, skills and approach. More general questions can help further exploration.

7.   Why have you applied for this job?

R1. *My present job gives me no chance to use my education and skills. The company has no idea how to use graduates. I have a lot more to offer, and I want the chance to do so.*

R2. *To tell the truth, my boss and I don't see eye to eye. We haven't quite got to the point of no return, but we soon will. I want to move on before matters get worse.*

R3. *From the advertisement, this job is exactly what I'm looking for, and I'm exactly what you're wanting. Your organization makes a fine product. I can offer top professionalism. Together we will make a winning team. Oh yes, and there's the money.*

R4. *The job you describe is one I can do, I will enjoy it, and know I can do well. My knowledge of your organization, from my contacts and from what I have read, tells me it is somewhere I would fit in particularly well. It would give me a chance to contribute, and to grow with the job.*

This complements question 6. If the reply to that does not provide much information you may need to follow up with question 7 immediately. Alternatively, you may prefer to use this question instead of question 6.

This is an area in which the attitude of the interviewer is as much on trial as that of the candidate. Everyone likes to be told how good they, the job and the organization are. But in reality people apply for jobs for both negative and positive reasons.

The negative reasons arise from discontent with the present situation (be it job or unemployment). Indeed, unless the candidates feel this, why should they go through the trauma of a job move? You may feel that some kinds of discontent ('lack of scope', 'poor prospects', 'no opportunity to use my skills', etc) are more acceptable than others ('I've fallen out with my boss', 'I've got myself into the wrong kind of work', 'I don't enjoy what I'm being asked to do'). However, these may all turn out to mask similar situations. Research shows that about half of all people seek other jobs because they are dissatisfied with their pay or some other aspect of their current job.

Therefore, if the reasons are honestly stated, they will almost always begin with the chance to be paid more, but interviewers conventionally tend to mark down those who admit this too readily. Most candidates will have rehearsed the line they think will be judged best.

You should try not to use this question as a means of getting compliments, and look carefully behind whatever form of words is used.

R1 conveys a touch of arrogance. Few organizations use new graduates as they would like to be used, especially in the early days. It is worth checking whether this is the first year since graduating; if not, you will need to go deeper. Other factors in your assessment will be the length of time in the job, and whether it includes, or is intended to include, an element of training. The transition from student to employee can be hard in even the most favourable circumstances.

R2 stands out badly, being entirely backward looking and negative. It does not glance once at the post on offer. But you could be wrong to reject a candidate simply because he or she is so frank about a problem that many have experienced. You should probe:

S. **This does happen. But are you just applying for anything to get away, and if not, why did you choose this job?**

R3 is confident in the extreme, and sounds as if it has been learnt from a book on how to succeed at interview. A supplementary may help the candidate to be more open:

S. **You sound more like a salesman. Would you like to tell me really why you want this job?**

R4 says all the right things, but you must note and compare with the other replies, such as those to the next two questions, before accepting it as valid evidence. There is a danger in appointing someone who is on top of the job from the start. While it is tempting to appoint someone who can 'hit the floor running', how long will it be before the job offers no challenge and they either move on or get bored and lose motivation?

---

8. What do you believe you can bring to the job?

R1. *I've done quite a few of the jobs before, over the years. I would need to learn the way you do things, of course, but so would anyone.*

R2. *I've got enthusiasm and drive. I'm a good team person. I learn fast, I'm loyal, hard-working and well motivated.*

R3. *Everything, from what you say. I'm doing a very similar job now, and I had customer contact in my previous job. Apart from the new documentation, I could sit down and get on with it now.*

R4. *I know about polymers both in theory, from my degree, and in practice, from my time in the Baxo Labs. I work with clients now and have a good track record in solving their problems. I'm a self-starter and I think I can show I'm creative.*

Some of the detail needed to substantiate these answers may have been covered by other questions. The probes below assume that this has not happened. The aspect of qualifications may be covered in the reply; if not, you may use question 9 in addition as a means of obtaining more evidence.

R1 sounds unenthusiastic and, if the candidate can express no more specific detail to such an important and highly predictable question, you may rightly wonder why the candidate applied for the job.

R2 is full of the most general words which, apart from making unsubstantiated claims, could be given whatever the job. You may wonder whether this candidate understood the person specification.

R3 offers no proof for its claims, and you must probe before judging. You should also ask yourself, as before, whether you want to appoint someone who would be on top of the job from the start:

S. **Will you give me a rather more detailed list of the similarities between this and your present job and then tell me how you see yourself progressing?**

R4 does rather better at offering detail, but would still benefit from probing:

S. **Please give me, very briefly, a couple of instances of the problems you've solved for customers.**

9. Which of your qualifications do you see as relevant to this post, and how?

R1. *Well, naturally, my degree in Computer Science, my membership of the British Computer Society and, as it's a management job, my NVQ (National Vocational Qualification) 4 in Management. I am also a member of the Institute of Management.*

R2. *I think my degree in English is relevant; although the subject isn't, the mental discipline and critical attention to detail is. I find debugging a computer program needs surprisingly similar thought processes to studying a sonnet by Shakespeare.*

R3. *I can't claim paper qualifications. I've learnt all I know on the job.*
R4. *All of them, really. As you see, I got my PhD (Doctor of Philosophy degree) in software development from the University of Woodburn. My MA (Master of Arts degree) from Bristol was actually awarded for a thesis on the application of database technology to the optimization of stock levels in retailing.*

These replies cover a complete spectrum.

R1 on the surface suggests the ideally qualified candidate. However, little information is given to provide the bridge between qualification and job. You will need to probe:

S. **Which parts of your degree course have you found of most value in your work, and how?**
S. **Has the NVQ actually improved your management in practice, and if so, how?**

For all of the replies you will need to state:

S. **It's company practice to see all qualifications before an offer of employment is made. I presume that wouldn't cause any difficulty for you?**

Studies have suggested that the proportion of qualifications falsely claimed by candidates is higher than might be thought.

R2 may seem to be stretching facts. However, there is nothing really wrong in this answer, as it is known that part of the reason for study at a higher level is to develop cognitive abilities. However, you will need to explore how these skills would actually be applied to the job:

S. **That's interesting. I don't know Shakespeare's sonnets as well as I would like, but please explain the similarity with debugging a program.**

R3 is frank, and further probing may tell you a lot about motivation, commitment, attitude to well-qualified colleagues:

S. **Have you ever considered getting a qualification by part-time study or distance learning?**

The answer to this may be the starting point for several probes or supplementary questions.

R4 is a fascinating answer. You may not have heard of the University of Woodburn. If this is the case, you should have checked its details before the interview. This would enable you to confirm the facts directly with the candidate:

S. **I'm sorry, but my knowledge of American universities is rather patchy. Could you tell me about Woodburn?**

This may bring a frank statement immediately.

R4. *Actually, University is a grand title. You send $1000 and they send you a great, big, garish certificate.*

S. **But you claimed it as a relevant qualification?**

R4b. *That's just my way of getting interviews.*

These responses are unlikely but demonstrate the ease of claiming qualifications. Candidates may claim awards from bogus colleges; they may falsely claim possession of real qualifications. As a responsible interviewer, it is your role to make sure that the qualifications are genuine. Use your local library to check up on qualifications and places of study.

10. **What do you** not **have that we need for this post?**

R1. *Well, I'm not sure that I could handle your computer system without training. Of course, I don't know about your product range. And I would have to get to know the people I would be working with, and the customers.*

R2. *Detailed product knowledge and experience of the company procedures.*

R3. *Nothing.*

The answers to the question can almost be evaluated by weight. Any candidate who produces a long list perhaps demonstrates lack of confidence. R2 is close to the right balance. R3 suggests a candidate who believes he or she has nothing more to learn. Is this self-deception, a poor attempt at guessing the expected answers or aimed at misleading you?

_____

11. **Imagine, for a moment, that you are appointed to this post, and that an extremely angry customer comes on the phone the first morning complaining that a large order, which has already been badly delayed, has now been incorrectly delivered. What, exactly, would you do?**

R1. *Well, er, I'd probably panic and look for your help.*

R2. *I would listen carefully, taking notes; explain I was new; promise to ring back quickly; get the full facts; seek your advice on company policy, and ring back at once with the appropriate answer.*

R3. *Make sure I didn't say too much. I suppose the best thing would be to ask the customer to put the complaint in writing.*

If the exploration of the candidates' previous experience has not given sufficient evidence of the individuals' skills in crucial areas of the job, you can explore these by posing hypothetical situations such as this.

R1 is weak in the extreme, even if it has the merit of frankness. You would be justified in probing further by saying:

S. **OK, but I may be out of the office. Then what would you do?**

R2 is an ideal answer. It needs probing to establish whether it is based on a textbook or experience:

S. **What's the nearest you've come to this in real life?**

R3 suggests defensiveness and lack of experience in customer service. It would certainly need exploration:

S. **How do you feel you would react to this approach if you were the customer?**

Expectations of rewards

Research suggests that many people seek to leave their current jobs because they are dissatisfied with the level of their pay or other factors relating to their conditions of employment. It does not, however, tell us what they seek from a new job.

It is known that money is a main motivator but other parts of the reward and benefits package matter as well – and some of these are not connected with pay. Interesting and challenging work is important, as is the opportunity to develop and progress. Employees want to feel that their efforts are valued and appreciated, and seek good relationships with colleagues and bosses.

As it is common practice to exclude salary information from advertisements, it is possible that candidates applying to your organization will not know how much you are prepared to offer. Similarly, they will not know what other benefits are on offer unless you tell them. One benefit of sending out information about the job before the interview is that you can give these sorts of details before meeting the candidates.

The candidates' CVs may include information about the salaries paid in their previous jobs and what benefits they received, especially if you ask for this to be included. However, not all candidates will be able to remember how much they earned in jobs they held 20 years ago, and is that information really relevant now? Some candidates may simply omit to give you the requested information.

Accepted wisdom suggests that it is unwise to appoint an applicant at a salary level lower than their current one. But the applicant may have good reasons as to why less money is acceptable to him or her. These could include moving to a part of the country where the cost of living is less, moving into a new area of work to change the direction of their career or for personal reasons such as a change in family circumstances. The only way to find out a candidate's reasoning is to ask him or her to outline what he or she seeks from the job.

When exploring financial aspects and personal reasons for moving, you will need to be cautious about invading the individual's right to privacy. Even if the salary on offer does represent a drop in income, there is little you can do to doubt the genuineness of the application if the candidate is fully aware of the implications and indicates that he or she is prepared to accept them.

_____

12. **Are you aware that the salary for the job is £X,000 per annum? How does this compare to your present salary?**

and

13. **You know what we're prepared to pay for the job. Would you be prepared to take it for that figure?**

R1. *I haven't thought about that, but I'm sure it wouldn't prove to be a problem.*

R2. *Something about the figure you mentioned is fine.*

R3. *Currently I'm on more than that. If I took this job, travelling would cost more and I would have added responsibility. I have been offered £3,000 more than your salary for a job which I also like the look of, so I'm really after no less than another £4,000.*

R4. *This may be a problem. I have been offered more already. I much prefer the job here, and was really looking forward to joining your team, but I can't altogether ignore the better offer. I do hope there is some scope for discussion on this.*

R5. *Salary is not the most important thing as far as I'm concerned. Job satisfaction and compatibility with the team I work with mean much more. However, I can't afford to lose too much, so I certainly would not come for less than I'm getting now.*

In view of the comments made above in relation to qualifications, it may be appropriate not to take the claims too seriously, although most will give some evidence.

R1 is an unlikely reply. However, from someone who is unemployed, you may be wrong to judge harshly. From someone apparently in a satisfactory job, it suggests other reasons for moving which may not have been discussed. In this case, you may probe:

S. **That is surprising. Most people at least have an idea of what they would like to earn. Are there any other reasons why you are looking for another job?**

R2 is cautious, probably indicating that the candidate is embarrassed. Prolonging the embarrassment is unlikely to achieve anything, unless other evidence (current salary, or some other remark) has given you reason to have doubts about salary. In such a situation, you must stick with it:

S. **You are quite sure about that? We both need to be clear where we stand on this one.**

R3 is pushing the boundaries. It may be a statement of fact, it may be a crude attempt to bargain, or it may be designed to impress you with the candidate's selling skills. You need to try to find out which:

S. **Oh, I'm rather disturbed to hear that. We have our own salary scales here, and have to think of our existing employees. We would have the greatest difficulty going above the published figure. It may be best if you accept the other offer.**

If the candidate maintains that position, it forces the decision, unless you really want to appoint the candidate and can justify exceeding the ceiling. You may feel it best to say so now:

S. **Well, in those circumstances, I guess there's not a lot of point in prolonging matters. Thank you very much for coming.**

The candidate may climb down, in which case you may choose to continue with the interview. Alternatively, the candidate may add something like R4.

R4 sounds genuine, and the response of a credible candidate. If your other evidence suggests that you may want to offer the job to this candidate, you are ready to further the discussion:

S. **Yes, it is a difficult position, but there may be some room for manoeuvre. Do you mind telling me about the other offer, and when you have to reply?**

The candidate may or may not enlarge much about the other offer, but if it is genuine he or she will say enough to show this. Certainly the urgency of the situation should be indicated, to which you may reply:

S.   **I see. I've noted that. Let's put it into cold storage until we've finished our other points, shall we?**

R5 is the classic reply. It is either from a book or a good candidate, but judging which will need the help of other data.

You may wish to close this section by finding out what else the candidate is seeking from the job. Questions similar to those given above will help you explore the candidate's expectations and hopes. Some of these may be pay related, such as a car, bonus and/or commission; others may be related to opportunities for further career progression. Some candidates may seek outcomes linked to factors such as challenging work or good working relationships. You may find the replies surprising, but if so, you should not show surprise.

Finding out what the candidate is hoping to get from the job and a new employer at this early stage is important, especially if you are not able to provide it.

seven

The **present: personal circumstances**

Overall objectives

1. To ensure that there are no factors which would make it difficult for the candidate to carry out the job required.
2. To seek additional indicators which might help to show the suitability of the candidate for the post.

There are various pieces of legislation that impact on the degree to which you can explore a candidate's private life and personal circumstances. Some of these laws have been in existence for many years, others are newly enacted; some have general application and others apply only to specific situations.

As an interviewer with responsibility for taking decisions on behalf of your organization, you have a duty and responsibility to be aware of the law and how it affects your conduct and to ensure that you do not commit any breach of it. This may seem an onerous responsibility, but it need not be so for if you apply some very basic principles and stick closely to good practice, the chances of falling foul of the law are considerably reduced.

Many of the statutes concern equity of treatment and the elimination of unfair bias. In practice this means that you should make sure that the person specification criteria focus on the factors required for effective performance of the job and not personal characteristics. If the selection process is designed to examine suitability against those criteria, you should have little cause for concern.

Much of the legislation that has been in force for some years aims to eliminate sex and race discrimination and it is illegal to discriminate between candidates on grounds of their gender, marital status, colour, race, religion and nationality. This legislation applies to all employers. The more recent legislation, which has extended the legal protection given to disabled people, applies only to employers with more than 15 employees. The Disability Discrimination Act 1995 requires these employers to make reasonable adjustments so that a disability should not bar a person from employment unless it would genuinely and significantly impede the individual from doing the work in question.

The Disability Discrimination Act does not prevent you from asking questions about a candidate's health and sickness record, but there is increasing evidence to suggest that it is difficult to predict future likely attendance on the basis of past medical history for anyone, able bodied or with a disability. Any questions should allow the candidate a chance to give reasons for their absences. It is possible that a disability may mean that the individual is likely to take more time off work than a fully fit colleague. In these circumstances you may wish to consider whether this is tolerable, given your resources and the nature of your business. Alternatively, allowing the individual to work from home or to make up the time over a period may be regarded as adjustments you could reasonably be expected to make.

Other legislation exists to prevent unfair discrimination against particular groups. This includes the Rehabilitation of Offenders Act 1974 and laws relating to Trade Union membership. There are plans to extend legislation to cover age discrimination by 2006. Detailed consideration of the law as it applies to recruitment and selection is outside the scope of this book, so sources have been listed in the Bibliography to provide more detail.

Interviewers, however, do need to be aware of the Human Rights Act, which was passed in 2000. While it covers only public bodies and for the most part excludes those organizations that are commercial or industrial in nature, many candidates will be aware of its provisions and expect its considerations to be applied to them. As with all new laws, clear interpretation is still awaited, but in the mean time it may be advisable to exercise caution, particularly in those companies that provide public functions. The Act provides:

- the right to respect for private and family life;
- freedom of thought, conscience and religion;
- freedom of expression;
- freedom of assembly and association.

It also prohibits discrimination on grounds of sex, race, colour, language, religion, political or other opinion, national or social origin, birth, property and status.

The safest way of complying with the legislation and so not contravening the candidates' rights is to ask questions that are directly related to the job and not to ask questions that may appear intrusive by being of a personal nature. Some advise that this is achieved by asking each candidate exactly the same questions and using a tightly prescribed script. This does not allow the necessary flexibility to probe or to follow up on areas that relate only to the one candidate. However, it is advisable to ask the candidates questions about the same areas of interest. When you need to explore a particular issue with only one candidate, you should make sure the link between the question, the job and the person specification is obvious.

It is also proper, within the confines of the legislation, for a prospective employer to explore with a candidate if and how other parts of their personal life may impact on their ability to perform the job to the standard expected. The following questions are here to guide your examination.

---

1. **I see that you stated in your application that you have suffered from back problems. Can you tell me how that may affect your ability to do the job as I have outlined it?**

R1. *It may be a little difficult for me to get in for the early starts, particularly when it is cold. I tend to be very stiff when I first get up and need some time to get going.*

R2. *It is mainly under control now, providing that I have regular physiotherapy and do my exercises.*

R3. *I need a special chair to support my back and have to make sure that I get up regularly and walk about. Then I have no real problems.*

R4. *It's difficult to say. My back can flare up without warning and then I need to have a few days of total bed rest. I don't know what causes it and my doctor says I just have to live with it.*

R1 may or may not present a problem. If the job requires all the staff to be available at the start of the work session, for example to take over from other staff or to open up to customers, then the candidate may not be able to satisfy an important requirement. However, if the work can be done on a flexible basis, it may be possible to accommodate the candidate's needs without too much effort.

The second and the third replies appear to be reasonable and can be confirmed through a medical questionnaire or examination, if your organization has these. Assistance and advice about aids and adaptations can be obtained from the Department for Education and Skills and in certain circumstances funding may be available to help with the purchase of special equipment or modifications, though under the Disability Discrimination Act you will be expected to carry out reasonable adjustments at your own expense.

R4 should ring alarm bells. It is unusual for an individual and his or her medical advisers to be totally unaware of the factors that trigger such levels of pain and discomfort. This demands further probing, possibly through a medical questionnaire and examination, for the candidate is suggesting that his or her attendance at work may be spasmodic and unpredictable.

You must resist the temptation to become a medical expert or instant psychologist. However, if you have reason for concern, you can rightly ask a potential employee to undergo a medical examination or provide an opinion from their General Practitioner about how their health or condition may affect their ability to do the job. Some employers do this as a matter of course. It is possible that some aspects of the health check will include confidential matters that do not concern you. However, you will be given information and advice from which you can form your opinion and make a decision.

2. **How much time did you have off work last year in addition to your holiday allowance and public holidays?**

R1. *None. I didn't even take all my holiday entitlement. We were just too busy to get it all in.*

R2. *I had to have several days because my son was having problems at school. But everything is sorted now and there have been no difficulties this term.*

R3. *I had a couple of days off when I had a bad cold last winter. The whole team was hit with it. And then I had a nasty stomach bug. That lasted over a week. My partner's company insists that everyone takes their holidays during the close down week, so I had to ask for extra days as I had used up all of my entitlement.*

R4. *Very little really. I remember having to have a couple of hours out of work to go to the dentist when my tooth broke as there were no emergency services available in the evening. But apart from that I find that I can manage to arrange everything for the evenings or I plan to take a day off.*

Attendance is one of the most difficult areas of managing people. Things do crop up that require attention and many services are not available outside normal working hours. But you should remember that employees are paid to come to work. It is not unreasonable for an employer to expect that they make arrangements wherever possible to organize other responsibilities around what they have agreed to do in their contract of employment.

R1, at first sight, may appear to be the answer of a hard working and committed employee whose previous employer placed unreasonable demands on the workforce. On the other hand, it may be the answer of someone who does not know when to stop. The increased incidence of stress is focusing on the importance of employees having enough rest from their work. You may wish to explore this reply further:

S. **Was the heavy work load caused by any particular reason?**

R2 appears plausible. Things do go wrong for children and parents may rightly need to intervene. Some probing will enlighten you a little more about how the candidate balanced their domestic and employment responsibilities:

S. **How did you organize your work around this?**

R3 may be the answer of someone hit with the usual type of work-place illnesses. But stomach bugs normally clear up in a few days and the need for extra holidays suggests a lack of planning. Further probing and possibly checks with the replies to other questions exploring the candidate's attitude to work may be merited.

R4 appears to be honest; things like this do happen. The candidate has supplied enough detail to appear to be honest and seems to be someone who can balance work and personal considerations. Whether this information is accurate can be confirmed by asking the previous employer for details of attendance.

---

3. **Are there any other personal factors or commitments that may affect your attendance at work?**

R1. *Nothing I can think of. There may be occasional domestic emergencies. A colleague had a burst pipe and had to wait all day for the plumber to turn up. But I don't really expect anything.*

R2. *Potentially. My parents are getting older and while they are very fit at the moment, I have to recognize that they may need to call on me more and more as I am an only child. Of course I will do everything I can to make sure that any impact on my work is kept to the minimum.*

R3. *Well, it's nothing really, but there have been times recently when I have had to help my brother out. He is trying to start his own business but can't afford to employ anyone else yet. He hopes to next month but while he is getting established he needs a hand from time to time.*

R1 and R2 appear to be realistic. It is possible that the candidate giving the first response may be giving you a hidden warning of problems to come. The second reply also contains a future warning but is given in a way that suggests that the candidate will plan, let you know what is happening and organize his or her life to keep responsibilities in balance.

R3 is concerning. You would be right to ask the candidate to make a firm commitment to the job if employment were offered:

S. **Can you guarantee that if you were offered the job, you would not do anything for your brother during your hours of work?**

The reply to this will enable you to decide how to proceed with the rest of the interview. Even when a positive response is given, you may need to keep the matter under observation if the candidate is employed. If the answer is not clear or in the negative, you may wish to terminate the interview there and then.

---

4. **I see from your CV that you are active in your professional body. Are you still the Meetings Secretary?**

R1. *Yes. I find that it is a very useful position to hold. There is only a small amount of work involved and I can do most of it in the evenings. The biggest benefit, in addition to going to the meetings, is that I get to talk to all sorts of really interesting people when I ask if they will come and speak to the Branch.*

R2. *Only for the next few months, as the AGM is due and I doubt if I will be re-elected.*

R3. *Yes. It is a role I find very rewarding in a number of ways. As well as personal satisfaction and development, I find the contacts I make can be beneficial for business purposes. I have been able to network with some very senior people who have helped me solve problems and put me in touch with other people in similar situations.*

Employers take very different views of their staff being involved in professional and trade organizations. Some see them as being good for business on a number of fronts in addition to networking. They provide another forum for the employer's name to be spread around, and staff can gain a broader perspective of the profession as well as developing useful skills. On the down side, it can be time-consuming and expose your good staff to those who prefer to poach rather than recruit.

R1 makes reference to the personal benefits gained from the candidate's involvement and can be seen as being reassuring in terms of time commitment. However, you may wonder what the employer gets back in return, for no matter how much the candidate does in an evening, there is bound to be some intrusion into the working day. A follow-up question is merited:

S.   **In what ways does this help you in your job?**

R2 is worrying. You might wonder why the candidate does not expect to be re-elected. Does this mean that the time commitment is excessive, that the candidate was not very good in the role and is being replaced, or that they did not enjoy it and are not standing for re-election? There is only one way to find out:

S.   **Why do you think that?**

R3 sounds very interesting, but you need to make sure that the candidate will do the job you employ them to do before embarking on the work for the professional body:

S.   **It sounds as if you might have more to offer us in addition to your skills and experience. But how much work is involved in being Meetings Secretary? Can you give an estimate of how many hours you spend on it each week?**

Outside interests and activities

When interviewing students and others who have not held a full-time job, it is especially important to gain an insight into the interests of the candidates, as they may have acquired skills and knowledge that might be relevant to the post to be filled. In such cases, these factors may provide some of the best predictors available, and this area of questioning should be pursued very thoroughly.

Exploring interests and out-of-work activities can also be valuable when interviewing people who are not currently in employment. Denied the outlet of a paid job, how do they use their time, energy and skills and seek self-fulfilment?

Candidates' outside interests can add significantly to your understanding and inform your assessment.

5. Tell me about your band.

R1. *Well, it's not mine really. I just go down and play the drums when the regular drummer's not there. It's an excuse for a good night out, really.*

R2. *Couple of my friends started it three years ago. Pete is our lead player, and Karen does the vocals. I play the guitar. We get quite a few bookings now.*

R3. *We call ourselves Week 13. Popular rock mainly, but we've worked out a sound of our own. I'm business manager; I find the bookings and make the arrangements. It's getting quite big; we're fully booked for six months and are making a recording next week.*

R1 and R2 do not help, hinder or suggest the need to probe further.

R3 sounds interesting, and could be positive or negative. The message is that the candidate has a strong entrepreneurial flair, which may or may not be tapped at work. Your reaction will depend on (a) whether the post in question might use such flair; and (b) whether it seems that the band might take time and energy that would be needed by the job, if appointed. Probing is required:

S. **How do you find time and energy for it all?**
S. **The post does involve some travelling, as you know. Might this create a problem?**

---

6. I see from your CV that you enjoy reading. What was the last book you read?

R1. *It's hard to remember. I get through so many. . . Mostly science fiction.*

R2. *I took* Sense and Sensibility *out of the library recently after seeing it on TV, but I found it quite boring after the first couple of chapters.*

R3. *I've discovered a writer called E V Lucas. He wrote a lot of essays about life during the First World War. It's only light reading, but it conveys the flavour of everyday life at the time really vividly; I feel I've been there almost. I've managed to put together a complete set of his books now.*

You are not assessing just anyone's reading habits with this question; you are discussing the reading of people who thought it worth putting 'reading' as an interest on their application. In doing this, they have implied that they see it as an activity of which they are reasonably proud and prepared to be questioned on. You are justified, therefore, in using their reply as evidence.

R1 suggests that 'reading' is a mindless activity that is pursued without purpose and that can be used to fill a blank space on the form and sound respectable.

If this is correct, it also implies the absence of other constructive spare-time interests. This may not, of course, be a negative factor. Many people with domestic commitments or demanding jobs have neither time nor energy for active leisure. But if none of these (or an equivalent) is the case, then you may wonder how the candidate views life in general.

R2 may or may not convey the same message as R1. *Sense and Sensibility* (or some other well-known title) may have been mentioned as a positive choice, in the spirit: 'Have you read it?' But it too might have been a cop out: 'The only title I can think of.' The probe is easy:

S. **I haven't read that for years. What else have you been reading recently?**

R3 sounds the sort of thing we are looking for: enthusiasm, positive choice, active understanding.

---

7. How do you find your magisterial duties fit in with work?

R1. *Not too much of a problem. We only have to do a certain minimum number of sessions a year.*

R2. *It takes about two days a month, on average, on regular days in the week. But we can also change days if we need to meet work requirements. Emergencies of one sort or another crop up occasionally. Does your organization have a policy on public service?*

The question of public service is one you must be clear on. Magistrates, councillors and other public appointments can make quite heavy demands on an individual and their employers' working time. Employers may take the view that, in allowing this, they are contributing to the effective running of the community of which their organization is part. They may feel there could be benefits in having a voice within the local establishment, or see this type of involvement as a valid way of developing the individual's skills. But, especially when choosing new employees, you may feel that such duties cannot be combined with effective performance in the job. This will, of course, depend partly on the nature of the job.

A realistic, consistent and clear view is essential, so that the new employee and others who may have to bear a share of the extra work all know where they stand. Grudging and partial acceptance will not work.

R1 is worrying, as it sounds rather like avoidance. The probe might be:

S.　**How many days did it actually take over the past 12 months?**

R2 throws the ball, correctly, into your court, and requires an answer. If your policy is not to encourage such activities, you will need to say so, adding:

S.　**In view of what I've said, how do you feel about your application for this job?**

The interview may terminate there, or you may receive an assurance, which must be noted and referred to in any subsequent offer letter, that the public duty will be limited or terminated, as your policy dictates.

8.　Has your Action Group succeeded in its aims?

R1.　*It hasn't really been very active. It started at a meeting last October, but I haven't heard anything for a month or two.*

R2.　*They wrote to the local councillors and our MP. They then got posters printed, and quite a lot were put out. But I'm not sure that anything has actually been changed. Democracy doesn't seem to mean much in our neck of the woods.*

R3.　*Not yet, but we've made some progress. We had the Minister down with some officials and we made a presentation to them. It went well, they promised to examine the case, and we got a lot of publicity out of it. There was a picture of the minister and me on the front page of the local paper. But there's a lot to do yet.*

Real involvement in local action demands much commitment, but is less likely to intrude on employment than holding a public office. The skills, determination and knowledge necessary to achieve any measure of success may sometimes overlap with the demands of the person specification. If this is true of the post you are filling, you may probe an activity such as this to gauge the depth of involvement and the likelihood of such commitment being turned into transferable skills:

S.   **How did you get involved with the Group?**
S.   **What has been your personal contribution to the Group?**
S.   **Have you done this sort of thing before? If you have, please tell me about it.**

---

9. How would the Drama Society get on if you accepted this job?

R1. *I'm sure they would find another Chair.*
R2. *That would have to sort itself out. My job comes first, and the Drama Society will survive without me – better, no doubt, than with me.*
R3. *There's a Vice Chair, who would be only too happy to take over. I should be sad not to see the move to our new theatre; we've put a lot of work into that. But I'm sure the project would not suffer; we always made a point of delegating and involving everyone. After all, I'll still be in the same country.*

The replies to this may have more direct relevance than the more personal questions. As the senior officer of the Society, the candidate will have a big responsibility for its success. The possibility of having to step down may indicate a lot about the candidate's level of loyalty and commitment more generally.

R1 is superficial and creates a negative impression. You may feel you should probe, for example:

S.   **How about the move to the new theatre you mentioned earlier?**

R2 shrugs the problem off. There is very little concern for the society and the closing remark suggests a possible rift.

R3 sounds considered, and gives the impression of planning how best to transfer responsibilities in an ordered fashion.

Self-image

Self-image is a valuable indicator of personality. How one person sees themselves may differ from the way they are perceived by others. But most people have a reasonably accurate view of their own strengths and weaknesses. The insight displayed and the way an individual describes themselves can also be good indicators of maturity.

But tools and time are limited, and any question you ask with this aim can only supplement the information obtained from the CV, the other sources and the references.

You should avoid trying to analyse candidates' personalities and playing the role of amateur psychologist. Making assumptions about motives can be dangerous as you will probably guess wrongly. When interviewing, your purpose is quite simple: you ask questions and gather sufficient evidence to enable you to make a prediction about the candidate's likely performance in the job.

When asking the following questions, you need to keep in mind the fact that some people undersell themselves, while others happily blow their own trumpet. Frequently women are guilty of the former and men the latter, but this is not always the case. You are advised therefore to check the information given against that obtained from other sources.

---

10. How might one of your closest and best friends describe you?

R1. *Ah. Well. Honest, friendly, helpful, good at my job. . . How will that do?*

R2. *I've never really asked them. Intelligent, conscientious, reliable, sometimes boring, but gets there in the end.*

R3. *Extrovert, energetic, ambitious, go-getting, definitely not over-modest.*

R4. *Highly articulate, creative, talks too much maybe, self-opinionated, very intelligent, arrogant occasionally, but usually manages to hide it.*

The replies to this question often show a surprising degree of insight, as far as they go. As with references from other people, what candidates do not say is often more revealing than what they do say.

The more the replies match the evidence you have gathered in other ways, the more likely they are to reflect the individual's self-image. When you hear an answer that contradicts other evidence, you must weigh the possibilities that the candidate lacks insight, that you have missed something, or that you are being given the answers that the candidate thinks you are seeking.

R1 will probably do very nicely, and lists most of what we ourselves would say in that candidate's favour.

R3 and R4 admit their own bias. What they say is probably right enough, but may not match the person specification.

R2 sounds plausible and can be compared to other evidence.

---

11. How might your worst enemy describe your character?

R1. *That's a tough one. I really don't know. Maybe that I was unambitious.*
R2. *May I plead the fifth amendment? No? I think I would be described as over-sensitive sometimes. Perhaps touchy on some subjects. But it would have to be admitted that I am superb at my job.*
R3. *I would probably be called a workaholic and accused of working too hard for my health. There's not much else to say.*
R4. *Inhibited, introvert, quiet, withdrawn. But that's wrong, of course.*

This question may be less revealing than the previous one. Perhaps surprisingly, candidates are happier at putting frank statements about their failings into the mouths of hypothetical friends than enemies. Nevertheless, you may gain additional evidence from some replies.

R1 probably clinches a view you had already formed.

R2 may add data you had not yet obtained, and is perhaps defensive in its jokey tone, suggesting a reluctance to answer honestly.

R3 is possibly a statement of the candidate's view of themselves.

The hypothetical enemy in R4 is almost certainly not wrong, despite the attempted disclaimer.

---

12. **Tell me something that makes you really angry.**

R1. *Not much at all. I'm really quite calm usually.*

R2. *I don't suffer fools as well as I should.*

R3. *I nearly said being asked a lot of personal questions, but luckily I stopped myself. Ha ha. Unnecessary delays, I think. Late trains. I'm a very impatient person.*

R4. *People who end by saying 'OK?' Yes, and excessive noise.*

These answers add a little more evidence to your assessment. You may feel you can believe all of them; everyone has something that irritates them. But as with other personal questions, you will not be told the whole truth; only what the candidate wishes to reveal.

R1 confirms the impression of a candidate who is able to exercise a degree of self-control. But this is a textbook answer and may merit a probe:

S. **Surely something occasionally makes you cross?**

R2 is probably truthful and may support other evidence.

R3 goes over the top. Such a flippant reply may suggest that the candidate is not taking the interview seriously.

R4 suggests someone who knows themselves reasonably well, but they would make an intolerant colleague. A follow-up question is needed:

S. **How do you deal with people who are noisy and say 'OK' a lot?**

eight

The **future**

Overall objectives

1. To explore the candidates' longer-term career plans (if any) and find out how the present application fits in.
2. To learn how the candidates intend to develop in the job and achieve their plans in the longer term.

The view candidates have of their future in the longer term may help your selection in several ways. It may show the degree of thought and personal planning and give additional insights into ambitions and expectations. Some candidates will not have formed detailed plans of how they see their career unrolling. It is not unreasonable to expect them to have some idea of how a move from their present situation into the job for which they are applying will help them make improvements to their working life and achieve their desired outcome better. It is also reasonable to expect them to have some broad goals, even if these only aim at avoiding certain types of work.

This is an area of particular importance with candidates such as students who are near the start of their career. With such people, it is reasonable to expect they have given some thought to the future. Also, in the absence of a track record, future plans will assume more importance than past achievement in providing evidence on which to base your selection.

Long-term career goals

While not everyone will have thought deeply about their long-term career objectives, accepting responsibility for one's own career has become more and more important. People are being encouraged to invest in their own development. If a candidate presents for interview without considering their longer-term future, you may rightly want to know why.

---

1. We've already discussed your career to date. What are your career objectives and plans for the future?

R1. *I want to get on. I want a job that is rewarding and pays the mortgage.*

R2. *I'm at a crossroads. I feel I have exhausted the scope of my career in computing, at least in this part of the world. The time has come for a new direction, and if it succeeds, well I've plenty of time yet.*

R3. *I've given this a great deal of thought and done a lot of research on it. There's no doubt in my mind that the future lies in plastics technology, and that's where I want to be. There's a shortage of the right people, and those who've got what it takes won't stand still long. I'm going to be one of those.*

R4. *I've decided to go further up the specialist ladder. I enjoy using the skills I have, and I want to develop and make the most of them. I need more qualifications to achieve what I have in mind. I've just started an MBA by distance learning. When I have that, in two years, I shall be ready for further experience and possibly promotion. After that, who knows?*

R1 says nothing that can help you positively. It suggests that the candidate has not given much serious thought to the subject and has provided a stock reply.

R2 tells a little more, although most of this would probably be evident from the CV or other replies. It includes nothing to suggest careful thinking and clear objectives. If you have not already been told about the wish to move away from computing, you may need to ask a supplementary question to find out what lies behind this decision.

R3 aims to create the impression of sensible analysis and deliberate planning. However, it sounds superficial, and lacks a direct link to the content of the job. It cries out for probing:

S. **How did you do your research?**
S. **What skills and qualifications will the 'right people' have?**

R4 is a considered answer. The plan is clear, and apparently achievable. It is based on achievements already made. The claims are (subject to checking) supported by the action of enrolling for the MBA course. The only danger in such an answer might be the one posed by the evident ambition. If appointed, will the candidate intend to move on within the two years, and if promotion is not available or achieved, will the individual end up discontented and frustrated?

2. How would this post fit into your long-term career plans?

R1. *It would be a good step up, and get me going again.*

R2. *It would broaden my experience, and give me the chance to prove myself in the direction I want to go.*

R3. *I believe it would be just right. It would use the skills I already have, but be sufficiently challenging to give the opportunity for development. With two or three years of this work under my belt, I believe I would have the right background for further growth.*

R4. *I've been hoping for the chance to work in your organization for a long time. The reputation it has for training its staff is second to none. Once someone has done well with you, the world is their oyster.*

This is not an easy question for the candidate. For many candidates, the truthful answer may be 'it pays more money' or 'it will get me away from an uncomfortable situation'. This is, of course, perfectly legitimate, provided that:

(a) the candidate is not just concerned with the money and has an interest in the job or your organization;

(b) the job offers more than a passing place on the way from an unsatisfactory situation into one that is more acceptable;

(c) you have been told the truth about the candidate's present position and the reasons for leaving it.

R1 is flat and of no interest. It leaves the feeling that the 'step up' might be more than the candidate could manage. It also leaves you wondering why the candidate needs to get going again, and going where?

R2 and R4 both cast the interviewer's organization in the role of a developer for other employers.

R2 creates the suspicion that the experience broadening may not really be part of a plan, but possibly the chance the candidate needs to recover lost ground.

R4 goes too far in its attempt to flatter. It also makes clear that the candidate would be looking outside again in the fairly near future. You want at least the show of commitment, however uncertain it might prove in the event.

R3 is a reasonable answer, managing to sound convincing, and you can note it and check against other evidence.

___

3. **If you were to get this post, how long would you expect to stay with us?**

R1. *That's very difficult to say. I hope we will develop a good relationship, and that I would be with you for many years.*

R2. *I'm a loyal sort of person, and I don't like changing more than I need to. If the job is as challenging as I'm sure it is, and the opportunities for development within your organization as great as I believe they are, it may well be a career-long commitment.*

R3. *Two years minimum in the job. After that, I shall be wanting to press on. But if I've understood you organization correctly, there'll be lots of headroom here for the right people.*

This question may sometimes be no more than the shadow boxing of interview convention, serving more to embarrass the candidate than to produce additional evidence, least of all about future intentions. But the replies may throw up something that will confirm or counteract the evidence you are gathering.

R1 is passive, and displays no drive or ambition. But there is a desire to please which may match the person specification. After all, if all your staff were wildly ambitious, the organization would soon be reduced to chaos.

R2 has fielded the question well, and in consequence you have learnt little or nothing.

R3 may ring warning bells, but is probably more brash than bad. As with the fourth reply to question 1, you may need to probe further:

S. **How will you feel if you are not able to make the sort of progress you seem to want?**

___

4. Where do you see yourself, jobwise, in five years' time?

R1. *I hope I will be a section leader by then. Maybe a manager like yourself.*

R2. *Five years is a long time. I hope that will give me time to realize most of my career goals. I would like to think I should either be a director or a consultant by then.*

R3. *Five years ought to give me time to grow within an organization that provides the right nourishment, such as I believe your own to be. I think that with the further training, and good management, I have it in me to reach Board level, I would hope within the manufacturing function.*

R4. *I would like to be head of my own, dynamically growing company. Selling my own widgets and knocking the spots off the competition.*

You have gained nothing from the question by receiving reply R1, except confirmation that that candidate sees a career as a gentle progression requiring little effort and less development.

R2 claims to have career goals, something you will need to check with previous answers or probe now:

S. **What exactly are your career goals?**

R3 adds the goal of growing within the manufacturing function, which could be important, the realization of the need for additional training and good management, combined with a touch of flattery. It adds up to a reasonably encouraging answer.

R4 is interesting, especially if you sell widgets. It suggests ambition and the candidate has made it clear that he or she intends to set up a company of his or her own. You must ask yourself whether you can deal with this degree of honesty and drive. Will the candidate be pushing at the boundaries and provide innovation, initiative and progress? You may need to explore the likelihood and consequences of individuals using your organization as a means of gathering experience and inside information before setting up their own businesses, possibly in competition to your own.

The answer offers the opportunity for a useful discussion. You must probe:

S. **That's fascinating, even a little frightening. Tell me how you would go about realizing this ambition.**

The reply, guided by further probes if needed, should help not only to assess how realistic the statement might be, but also to show more of the interests and strengths of the candidate.

---

5. **If you were to be appointed to this post, do you feel there would be any additional qualifications or courses of study that might be helpful to you, and if so, which?**

R1. *Not really. I would want to concentrate on picking up the job.*
R2. *In the course of time, yes. I think training in structured programming would be particularly helpful, and I would like to go on a course to learn about advanced software design.*
R3. *Well, yes. I understand your organization sometimes sends people on MBA courses at Harvard. This is one of the reasons I'm so keen to work for you.*

This question is highly predictable and one for which the candidates should have a prepared answer.

R1 is a steady response but suggests little preparation. It contains no recognition of the need for ongoing development other than that to be gained from experience or the possibility of future changes.

R2 sounds more thoughtful and positive, and is credible.

R3 may appear to push too far. Even if you do send people to a business school as prestigious as Harvard, the chances are that factors additional to an individual's ambitions would influence your choice of participant.

The link between career and private plans

This takes the investigation of the future a stage further and probing it will give you some evidence of the candidate's quality of thought and longer-term planning. However, take care to respect the candidate's right to privacy.

---

6. The interaction between career and outside interests is often a problem. How would you like to see these fitting together in your own long-term life plans?

R1. *You are right. I understand the need to keep work and play in balance. It is important to take breaks and do something different in the evening and at weekends. But then there are times when work has to come first; when deadlines are pressing or difficulties arise. But overall, I think I can manage to keep both my personal interests and my career on an even keel.*

R2. *My work comes first, of course. But I'm Chair of the Community Association this year, and I don't want to let them down if I can help it. That's why I'm looking for something that will not make too many demands on my spare time.*

R3. *I decided a long time ago that my career comes first. As long as that is going well, other things will go well, and can be fitted around it. This seems to have worked so far, and it remains my strategy.*

R4. *I have had to think carefully where my priorities lie. When I started work, I had to decide whether I wanted to sacrifice my personal life for a star-studded career. Even though I had ambition and wanted to do well, I also wanted to have a family life. I have seen during my childhood just how much damage can be caused by an absent parent and I did not want to repeat the mistakes made by my parents. I decided that I would aim for a balance.*

In practice, this has meant being strict about the divide between home and work, and I think I have so far been successful in achieving this. I have found that my career has not been meteoric; nevertheless I have made progress and have had some very interesting experiences. I also seem to be able to avoid the stress that some of my previous colleagues have suffered. This may be because I am able to keep my job in perspective. I always meet my deadlines and targets, yet find the time to relax and enjoy playing a full part in family life.

Candidates will usually claim that their career comes first, for obvious reasons. Among these replies, R1 is too vague to interpret clearly, and although R2 makes a statement about this, the remainder of what is said simply serves to cast doubt on it.

R1 indicates no clear thinking or planning. It suggests an easy-going approach.

R2 implies that the stated order of priorities ('my work comes first') is not the real one. The Community Association appears to be the current priority. You may not welcome this, especially if the post in question calls for long hours or travel. On the other hand, it suggests strong commitment and a good level of achievement in a spare-time activity. Replies to other questions may indicate why this is so, what it tells you about the candidate, and the chances of the post in question tapping these skills and interests.

R3 is simple and straightforward, but, as with R1, gives very little detailed evidence; other evidence will help to indicate its credibility.

R4 seems the reply of someone who actually has thought things through, and who has taken account of the impact work can have on other commitments and responsibilities. It conveys a sense of an application being made as a genuine part of a careful plan.

---

7. What would be your reaction to someone who suggested backing you in setting up your own business?

R1. *I would be flattered, but I doubt if I would pursue it. I have been too long as an employee. It wouldn't be practicable at my stage of life.*

R2. *I should be tempted to go for it, if the offer was real.*

R3. *Utter amazement, I think. I believe I am a professional, and have a great deal I can contribute to the right organization, but I'm not an entrepreneur, and don't want to become one. For me the solid and, I hope, inspired professionalism; for someone else the risk-taking.*

R4. *Not today; I'm not ready. But in five or so years, that could be possible. I've a lot to learn from, and a lot to give to, other organizations for a long while yet, but one day that may be exactly what I'm after.*

Drive and entrepreneurship are not the same, but it is unlikely you will find the second without the first. If these are requirements included in the person specification, you will need to assess the replies to the question according to which best displays them.

R1 probably doesn't help. It may quite well be a reasonable statement in the candidate's circumstances, but it gives the impression of an individual disinclined to take risks.

R2 is too thin to say anything by itself. If supported by other answers, you may be inclined to accept it on face value, or think it worth a probe:

S.   **How would you go about it?**

R3 is a more considered and complete answer, but only tells you that the candidate's drive is better assessed by replies to other questions.

R4 suggests that the candidate is open to alternative ideas but recognizes the need for a planned, calculated approach. This is something you can note and compare with other replies.

nine

The **awkward candidate**

Candidates, even though they are apparently seeking a job, are not all angels. They may display any number of seemingly negative features. You may feel that those who do this do not deserve consideration. But some of these faults may have no relevance to the person specification, some may be purely temporary, and some may have been brought on by the tension of being interviewed.

You can develop techniques that will help overcome any awkwardnesses. These will also help you develop your skills and confidence as an interviewer, as interviewers can also experience nerves.

The problems you may see in candidates include:

1. shyness and talking too little;
2. talking too much;
3. excessive nerves;
4. trying to dominate;
5. using physical attraction;
6. evading the issue;
7. lying and unacceptable deceit.

Shyness and talking too little

If you failed to obtain sufficient information from a candidate, it may be that you were responsible. You should review all you have done, said or failed to do or say that might be the cause of the problem. You might have:

- failed to introduce someone present: possibly you did not explain your role or did not explain why the other person was present;
- asked a difficult or embarrassing question before rapport was fully established;
- said something without realizing it that has puzzled or upset the candidate;
- talked so much that the candidate felt that he or she was not really expected to say very much;
- overwhelmed the candidate with an excess of information, even though you thought it all relevant;
- cowed the candidate by expressing your own strongly held views on a particular subject.

Teenagers and entrants

The very worst problems tend to occur with some teenagers, who may be at a time in their personal development when relating to any adult is difficult. Similarly, others with no recent experience of the workplace may find an interview intimidating.

The form of the questions and way in which they are asked are even more important with shy people than with other candidates. Most, when posed a closed or yes/no question, will enlarge on their answer without further prompting; shy people will not, and you may be faced with an unending string of monosyllabic answers.

The best starting point is to get the candidate talking on *anything*, however irrelevant. You should start with one of the candidate's declared interests or experiences.

1. **You have given watching football as one of your hobbies. Which team do you support?**
2. **I see that you are involved in your local school. What exactly do you do there?**

If no interests have been shown on the CV, it is probably *not* effective to probe. A question such as:

3. **What do you do with your spare time?**

may be resented, or draw an answer such as:

R1. *Oh, not much. Watch TV, go round to friends, that sort of thing.*

But you should only follow up a leisure interest if you have some knowledge of and interest in the subject. You may find yourself in the midst of a detailed conversation on a subject you know very little about and which is not really relevant to the interview. Young people in particular dislike being patronized and pick up on it with lightning rapidity.

Whether this approach has helped or not, the move to the next area of questioning must be approached with great care. A wrong choice, or too sudden a transition, may spoil anything already achieved. School or college is often a relatively easy subject for young people, and has the added advantage that they are likely to see it as something in which you may have a legitimate interest. But exam results, even if good, are a conversation stopper. You might try:

4. **Why did you (not) stay on?**
5. **What projects did you do in your last year?**

For older people, you will have to find other topics, for example:

6. **Did you do any courses?**
7. **Did you think about doing some voluntary work?**

As in any interview, encouragement will help, if you can find the right way to give it. Apart from positive body language and the best selection of encouraging noises, you can try such comments or questions as:

8. **That is most interesting. Will you tell me some more about that please?**
9. **Am I making my questions clear for you?**
10. **Good, excellent, please go on.**

The replies do not matter as such, as these are opening questions designed to lead into the main body of the interview.

Talking too much

Interviewers often assume that candidates will have to be encouraged to start talking, but this is not always the case. Nerves or basic character may cause some to be almost unstoppable. With experience, you will be able to pick this up fairly early on.

11. **We are getting rather short of time. May we pass on, please?**
12. **Am I right in thinking you have said. . . [then give a brief summary]? Good. Now can we talk about the next topic?**
13. **Do you always enjoy talking about. . . [the topic] so much?**

The replies to the questions given above are unimportant. What we want is to maintain control over the interview.

Other ploys available include such old faithfuls as:

- referring to your papers;
- breaking eye-contact;
- stop taking notes;
- checking your watch;
- bringing in one of the other interviewers.

Failing success with any of these, you will be driven to say simply:

14. **I'm sorry, but time is beginning to run out and there is another candidate waiting. Can we start to bring matters to a close?**

Excessive nerves

Excessive nerves may show in too much or too little talking. The many other ways they may show include:

- trembling, especially of the hands;
- sweating;
- tapping of the feet;
- tense, tight or unnatural posture;
- frequent changes of posture and shifting of weight;
- clenching of the hands or gripping furniture;
- failure to make eye-contact;
- talking too fast;
- talking very quietly, or replies that tail off into inaudibility;
- failure to listen to the question;
- losing the thread of what is being said.

All interviews generate tension in the candidate (not to mention the interviewer). But there is a temptation to believe that anyone who shows excessive nerves must be a poor candidate. This may be correct, if the person specification for the job involves the ability to do well in interview-type situations, as with one-to-one selling, or meeting people in a similar situation. But if this is not the case, as is most unlikely with, for example, a VDU operator, a ledger clerk or a research chemist, you will need to help the candidate deal with his or her nerves so that you can obtain the necessary information.

15. **Which was the period in your career you enjoyed most? Please tell me a little about it.**
16. **Tell me something about your photography.**
17. **From what you say in your CV, you must have enjoyed your time at university. Please tell me about it.**

The way forward

In this situation, the replies to the questions do not matter as such.

Until tension has lessened, the questions should concentrate on aspects you believe the candidate feels positively about, and which pose little or no threat. There are plenty of these to be covered in any interview.

The form of the questions should be as open as possible and you should take care about your body language and the way you ask the questions. A fixed stare, forward lean and rapid-fire questions will do little to ease nerves.

The impossible

Sometimes the relationship between interviewer and candidate just does not work – the chemistry is wrong. If it seems that you are in this situation, you will need to realize it and do something about it; to soldier on regardless will achieve nothing.

Having other interviewers present can help, for you can quietly take a back seat and allow other members of the panel to ask most of the questions. There is nothing wrong in passing a short note to one of the others to brief them on what has happened.

However, if you are not able to establish any degree of rapport during the interview, you must think seriously about what this would mean if the candidate were to be offered the job. It would be right to discuss with the other interviewers, at the end of the interview, how they felt they were able to relate to the candidate. If they experienced no difficulty, you would need to consider why you and the candidate failed to connect. If you will be the manager of the person appointed, this failure could be indicative of a disastrous working relationship.

If the other interviewers experienced similar problems, you might take this as evidence of the candidate's poor social skills. If the job is part of a team or customer service skills are important elements of the person specification, you may wish to view the candidate's suitability in the light of your direct experience.

Trying to dominate

A few candidates see the interview as an opportunity to 'hard-sell' themselves. You should always listen and try to be as fair as possible. They may try to browbeat you, pressurize you, dominate you or take control of the proceedings. You cannot allow this to happen. As interviewer, it is essential that you remain in control, while allowing the candidate to present him- or herself to the best of their ability.

18. **Forgive me, but we need to stick to the interview plan. OK?**
19. **Thank you for your views. May we go back to my question now please?**
20. **I want to be fair to all the candidates, so there is certain ground I must cover with each. Do you have any objections to discussing your experience when you worked for Browns?**

Questions may prove ineffective in such a situation, and you may soon move to firm statements.

21. **I'm sorry, but we have very limited time. I must move you on quickly to the next point.**
22. **I'm sorry to interrupt you there, but if I am to consider you for this post, there are certain things I must know. The question I asked is one.**
23. **If you are not prepared to tell me about your experience, we appear to be wasting each other's time. Thank you very much for coming. Let me show you out.**

Fortunately, such situations do not arise very often.

Using physical attraction

The importance of establishing rapport during the interview has already been mentioned several times as it is important as a foundation for any subsequent working relationship. A normal human characteristic is the wish to be with people we like and who are like us. When first meeting a new person, the first aspects to be assessed are that person's physical characteristics. This assessment takes place in seconds, often at a subconscious level.

The candidates' physical appearance, stance and demeanour, their clothes, hairstyle and jewellery, and use of cosmetics and perfume all combine to create an image that becomes fixed in the interviewer's mind. Changing that first impression can be difficult as there is a tendency to seek further evidence to confirm it and to discount any that attempts to disprove it.

Some candidates are aware of this process and deliberately set out to exploit their physical attributes, believing that this will help them demonstrate that they are more suitable for appointment than the other candidates. Fortunately, this does not happen very often, but you do need to be aware of the traps that are being laid for you.

The interview is a closed meeting deliberately set up to enable the candidates to impress potential employers. Some candidates will use every tool at their disposal. Of course, candidates will dress to impress, but there is a difference between being well turned out in the accepted garb of the world of work and being dressed for the kill.

The nature of the questions that need to be asked, for example about experience, reasons for leaving a job and interests, can lead to an atmosphere of confidentiality and intimacy. This could tempt the candidate to reveal inappropriate information or to be over familiar.

You need to be aware of what the candidate is doing and to guard against your natural tendency to be influenced by initial impressions. Nevertheless, what the candidate does and apparently intends to do provides you with additional information. Therefore, when making decisions about suitability for the post you need to be aware of the impact personal preference may have in relation to unfair discrimination. You will most likely avoid this by focusing clearly on the needs of the job.

A case was taken to an employment tribunal by a man claiming that he had suffered sexual discrimination because he was denied employment as a result of his beard. His case was not proven, for the job in question involved serving food and the company had a strict dress and appearance code in force. But often the issues are not as clear cut as this and all interviewers must take care not to allow their prejudices and use of stereotypes to influence their assessment of a candidate on factors not set out in the person specification as relevant to the job.

Training and experience of interviewing, especially with inter-viewers who have had considerable experience themselves or professional training, are the best ways of preparing to deal with such awkward candidates. Interviewing with other people also helps to avoid any unfounded accusations. Note taking is essential as the record of the meeting will provide evidence that can support your memory if any claim is made against you.

The most important safeguard is a well-prepared and detailed person specification that has been drawn up on the basis of job analysis and can be clearly related to the job's requirements. Obviously the visible use of this document during the interview will tell the candidate that you know what you are looking for. Physical attractiveness, unless contained in the person specification, is not one of the factors.

Evading the issue

You must recognize deliberate evasion as soon as you meet it. It is wasting your time. Useful techniques in such a situation include:

Giving time to focus. You must accept that most candidates need time to focus on a question, and usually feel the need to talk while they are doing so. It takes a strong candidate to remain silent in an interview while thinking. The pressure to rush into speech is great, so you must allow space, especially if you are trying to get the flow going smoothly. Patience on your part is essential and will save time in the end. You also need to appreciate that some candidates may misunderstand a question, possibly as a result of nerves, and give another answer. If this happens, gently stop the candidate and repeat your original question.

Asking if it is deliberate. Some evasion is quite unconscious; the result of a woolly thought process, a bad choice of words, or a poorly worded question. You will need to decide if any of these are the case, and react accordingly. You may build it into your assessment of the candidate and pass on. If the subject is important, or the fault with your question, you should ask a differently worded question on the same subject.

Avoiding interruption. Interruption in particular is unhelpful, and you should do it only rarely and when quite unavoidable. Questions like 27 should be very infrequent. If you find you have interrupted a candidate more than twice, something is going wrong, and you should ask yourself (possibly the candidate) what it is.

24. May we just go back to that one please? I'd like to hold on to my original question for a moment.
25. Forgive me, but I must press this point. What I would like to know is exactly *why* you made that decision.
26. We seem to have wandered off the subject. May I bring you back to my question, which was what you saw as your greatest problem in that assignment?
27. Sorry to interrupt, but time presses. I must move you on to your next post, head of development. What were your responsibilities in this?

Taking tough action. If evasion continues, either in one lengthy answer or over a long sequence of replies, you may feel that you must act firmly.

28. No, that doesn't answer my question. Please try again.
29. I sense you are reluctant to answer my question. Am I right, and if so, why is this so?

Lying and unacceptable deceit

As in normal life, there is in interviews a thin and sometimes uncertain dividing line between acceptable and unacceptable deceit.

Some candidates will bend every situation as far as it will go to what they see as their advantage. Interviewers should expect them to do this, and the whole process of selection interviewing should be designed to take account of this.

Some things are not acceptable, however. These include misstating material particulars, such as:

- claiming false qualifications;
- claiming incorrect salary levels;

- incorrectly claimed periods of employment;
- misstating age;
- hiding dismissal or forced resignation;
- hiding criminal convictions, unless expired, as provided for under the terms of the Rehabilitation of Offenders Act.

You must not worry unduly about the items on this list, not because they do not matter, and not because they will not happen, but because they are difficult to check at interview. However, you can develop a nose for such things, for example spotting inconsistencies or repeated avoidance of questions relating to a particular experience or period of time. The use of techniques such as those listed below can be helpful to confirm factual details:

- a good application form, which includes all relevant questions and the warning that material misstatement may lead to dismissal if appointed;
- sight of all relevant documents, including birth certificate, passport and/or qualifications, before appointment;
- careful taking-up of references, in writing.

The grey areas

Some areas are on the borderline, and may be acceptable or not depending on how they are expressed, how far they are pushed, and how they match with other aspects. These include:

- overstating responsibilities;
- incorrect statement of reporting lines;
- overclaiming of achievements;
- hiding serious problems.

These may, at least partly, be picked up at interview, if you have studied the paperwork carefully and questioned thoroughly, listening to, noting and comparing replies and probing when unsure.

Three kinds of clues may help.

Internal inconsistency. You must always be alert to the details of what was said, and how answers to different questions match up. If you have any doubt, you must probe:

30. You say you found management interference frustrating, yet I have a note that you told me earlier that you had bottom-line responsibility for the operation under the Board. What do you mean?
31. Sorry. I understood you to say earlier that you reported to the manufacturing director, but now you say your plan was blocked by the plant manager. Can you explain just what the chain of command was?
32. Why were you moved sideways, having just improved profitability by over 100 per cent, as you have told me?
33. I'm afraid I don't understand why you decided to leave without another job to go to, only six months after joining if, as you say, there were no problems in the job. Can you enlighten me?

Inherent improbability. Common sense and your own experience must never desert you, even under the charm of a convincing candidate.

34. It is very unusual for a new graduate to be given 'total responsibility' for such a large operation in their first appointment. Can you elaborate on exactly what that responsibility covered? Who did you report to, and what were that person's responsibilities?
35. You say you were one of 18 development engineers. Surely you didn't all report directly to the Research and Development director?
36. If the conference was the success you tell me, why was it never repeated?
37. That seems an odd time to change jobs, just after a major success and a big increase in responsibilities. What had happened?

Special knowledge. Occasionally, you may be in the happy position of knowing more than a deceitful candidate expects.

38. **Why did you leave Aberdeen University after only three years, when the degree course there lasts four?**
39. **I thought all Cambridge graduates became Masters in time?**
40. **I'm sure my colleagues at Smiths would be most interested to learn of your responsibility for the success of that operation.**

The **final stages**

Overall objectives

1. To answer the candidate's questions.
2. To give the candidate an opportunity to add further information.
3. To check that the candidate still wishes to be considered.
4. To make clear what the remaining stages of the process are.
5. To leave a good final impression with all candidates.
6. To pick up any final information.
7. To offer the post to the chosen candidate, and to inform rejected candidates.

This list may look long but all items, except perhaps the first, are usually brief.

Answering the candidate's questions

The candidate will have had several opportunities to ask questions, including during the introductory phase (Chapter 4, page 77) and the discussion of the present post (Chapter 6, page 109). However, it is essential that the candidates are given this final chance. Additional questions may have been raised as the interview progressed, or there may be points the candidate did not have the opportunity to discuss. It is better to deal with these rather than leave matters unresolved.

You must ensure that you have allowed sufficient time for this phase to be completed without undue haste. The amount of time needed may vary with the seniority of the post. It will also be influenced by how much information you send out about the job, and the organization. If this has been comprehensive, you might find that only two or three minutes will be enough, as most points are likely to have been covered.

1. Are there any points you are still not clear about, or any questions you would like to ask me, before we finish?

R1. *No, nothing, thank you.*

R2. *Can you tell me about the perks? What would I get above the basic salary? Would I be paid for overtime? Does the job rate first-class travel? And the car; what models could I choose and would I get private mileage?*

R3. *We've covered nearly everything I wanted to ask, but there are just a couple of points. First, I'm not clear exactly what authority the post would have for recruiting and training staff. Second, perhaps you can enlarge on the relationship between this post and the marketing director; is there a direct line, functional responsibility, or a purely advisory relationship?*

R4. *Can you give me a salary indicator, please?*

Conventionally, recruiters judge replies to this question by two standard criteria.

First, the candidate is expected to have some questions left to ask; if not, this can be seen as an indicator of the candidate being less than seriously interested. This may not, however, be fair or right. It is perfectly possible that the interview has been so comprehensive as to cover all the points that a seriously interested candidate might have.

Second, undue emphasis on salary and perks is often judged to be bad. The candidate should, according to this view, be principally concerned about job content and satisfaction, and think little about the quid pro quo. Clearly there is some truth in this, but it is a matter of balance, and will vary widely according to what information has already been made available.

If you have given no indication, for example, about salary, a question about this is not only reasonable, but indicates the candidate's serious intentions. On the other hand, questions about the fine details of other rewards do not sound good.

R1 fails the first test, but, for the reasons given above, to mark it down in the absence of other evidence may be unfair. If, however, it comes at the end of a passive and unconvincing display, in which some important angles have *not* been covered, you would be justified in taking it as further evidence of weakness or lack of interest.

R2 concentrates on the fine detail of pay and monetary rewards. There are no job-related questions or questions about development. You may wonder how much 'give and take' the candidate would be prepared to offer and accept.

R3 would conventionally be seen as a good answer. It appears to show that the candidate's main concerns focus on the post and its responsibilities. However, convincing sounding questions are one of the easiest things to plan and rehearse when preparing for an interview. How much faith you pin on such a reply will depend on how it matches the evidence you already have.

R4 will be interpreted according to the amount of information you have already given in the advertisement and during the interview. If you have given little or none, it is highly relevant, and not to ask it might indicate lack of serious interest, an over-anxiety to please, or perhaps undue timidity. But if you realize after the end of the interview that salary has not been discussed, you will probably wish to pick the point up yourself.

---

2. **By the way, I don't think we've discussed salary. If we were to offer you this post, it would be somewhere in the range of 25 to 27k. How do you feel about that?**

R1. *Fine, no problem.*

R2. *As you know, I'm on 22k at the moment. From what I have learnt of the job, I do see it as a clear increase in responsibility – one that I welcome very much – and I would like to hope that you would be prepared to appoint at the top end of that range.*

R3. *Well, I've been looking through the ads for other jobs of this type, and the going rate is somewhere between 30 and 35k. I saw one in the* Sunday Times *at 38k. Admittedly it was in London, but in other ways it was identical to yours. It was this kind of remuneration I was looking for when I applied, and knowing the reputation for fairness your organization has, I felt sure you wouldn't let me down.*

R4. *Not happy. You didn't state a salary in your ad, but the fact you called me to interview seemed to suggest that you would be prepared to offer a good rise on my present pay. Unless you are able to go up to at least 30k, I'm afraid I must withdraw.*

The way the question of pay is approached will depend to some extent on custom and practice in the organization. Public bodies advertise their rates openly but may be generally less able to negotiate than the private sector. It will also depend on the amount of information on pay already supplied to the candidates and the stage reached in the selection process.

However, nothing can be gained by continuing the process if agreement on pay is unlikely to be reached, so you should be prepared to discuss the matter whenever it is raised.

How you interpret R1 will depend mainly on the candidate's present salary, if any. If you can offer a reasonable rise, or if the candidate is unemployed, the reply is quite straightforward. If, however, there is no increase, you may wonder why the candidate is prepared to accept the post. You may wish to seek an explanation:

S.   **I'm afraid that means we would have to start you on a little less than you're getting now. What would you feel about that?**

R2 appears reasonable and deserves a response that reflects the amount of flexibility you have to set the starting salary, your keenness on the candidate and the stage reached in the process:

S.   **Yes, I will note that point, and if we decide to offer you the post, we will certainly do what we can.**

R3 sounds like a crude and premature attempt to put on negotiating pressure, and may well be met by a fairly firm, possibly negative response:

S.   **I'm afraid this is not the moment to negotiate terms. All I can say is that we will offer what we see as a fair salary to whoever we choose.**

R4 is clearly terminal, unless you feel the candidate is highly suitable. If you do, you may revise your ceiling there and then. If you do not, you may have to accept the closure:

S.   **I'm sorry you feel that. Unfortunately, we are not able to go higher, as that would impact on our existing people. If that is your feeling, there is no alternative but to thank you for coming to see us and wish you well in your search for a suitable opening.**

Final information

There is nothing worse than the feeling, as soon as you have stepped outside the interview room, that you *should* have remembered to say so-and-so, or the regret that you were never given a chance to tell the interviewers about your proudest moment.

By the same token, the interviewer who helps a candidate to avoid such feelings will leave an impression of fairness and consideration in the latter's mind, and may also pick up useful pieces of evidence that would otherwise have been missed.

3.   **Before we finish, are there any points that we haven't given you the chance to make, or anything else that you would like us to bear in mind?**

R1. *No thanks.*
R2. *Only to say thank you for a very fair interview and that I hope I am offered the job.*
R3. *As I see it, you are looking for someone who can combine bookkeeping and computer literacy with good management experience, plenty of drive and potential for further development. While, as I said, it is a year or two since I last did any bookkeeping I believe I fit your profile exactly, and the post you are filling would enable me to use my skills and experience to full advantage. I would make a real contribution to the success of your organization. Thank you very much for your time, and I look forward to meeting you again, soon.*
R4. *Well, when I answered your question about the way we tackled assignments, I think I may have given the impression that we were*

171

sometimes rather superficial. If I did, I would like to correct it; in fact, we are always very thorough. I'm afraid I didn't choose my words well in that answer.

R1 cannot be faulted as it stands. It may, however, be confirmatory evidence of a lack of interest.

R2 is also polite and reasonable, but may indicate that the candidate feels that he or she has not performed to their best.

R3 summarizes the candidate's view of his or her own strengths. This may be different from your view and, depending on how the words are said, it may come over sounding like a 'hard sell'. This is a legitimate enough aim on the part of the candidate, and this attempt is clear evidence of good selling ability, something which may well figure in the person specification.

With R4, the candidate has accepted your invitation, and you must resist any temptation to find fault with him or her for doing that.

How you assess the reply will depend on how closely it matches your own perception of what happened during the part of the interview mentioned. If you did form the impression described, you might give credit both for the substance of the correction and for sensitivity. If you did not, or the candidate has missed the point in some way, this may be a final indication of interview nerves.

Is the candidate still interested?

You must not assume that, having met and talked at length to a candidate, he or she will remain interested in the post. As was said at the beginning, selection must be a two-way process. You will save much time, and possibly avoid the loss of alternative candidates, if you check the strength of the candidate's interest before closing the interview.

4. **Can I take it that you do still wish us to consider you for this post?**

R1. *Oh, yes please.*
R2. *Yes, I think so.*

R3. *Certainly. Having had this chance to meet you and learn more about your operation and what the post will entail, I am even keener than before. I am certain that this is the opportunity I am seeking.*

R4. *I have a doubt. The line of responsibility through the site manager is not what I had expected. Unless I have misunderstood in some way, my feeling is that I shall have to go away and think what it might mean in practice.*

R1 adds very little, except perhaps a degree of enthusiasm, unless you expected a negative answer, in which case you will have to probe:

S. **You surprise me. From what you have said, I felt we had come to the mutual conclusion that the post was not what you were really looking for. Can you enlighten me?**

R2 sounds weak when real conviction was called for. It cannot be passed over. But the probing may need to be gently done, or the doubts may be covered up again quickly, and you could waste time and effort making an offer which is refused. You might try:

S. **You sound a little unsure. Perhaps there is some aspect I can help you with now, while we are still together?**

R3 sounds good, but is easy to rehearse and say. You must compare it with the impressions you have already built up.

R4 must be followed up. It might be no more than a manoeuvre to draw you into a premature and favourable decision. How you follow it up will depend on how keen you are on the candidate, how accurately the position has been understood, and how much flexibility you have.

If you see the candidate as a serious contender, and the relationship has been understood correctly, you may ask:

S. **What is there about this arrangement that concerns you?**

Depending on the reply, you may continue:

S. **That is how it is at the moment. I'm sorry if it creates some doubts. However, if that is your only concern, may I suggest we leave it for now? We have other candidates to see. Perhaps**

we can discuss this again if we decide to take your application further.

Remembering that the candidate has decisions to make, it is not unreasonable for one to ask for time to think, especially if new information has been given during the interview. The offer of employment is often a negotiation and an extension of the interview. In these circumstances an appropriate closing sentence would be:

S. **That is the situation, certainly, but we may be prepared to discuss adjustments with whoever we wished to appoint. May I say we have noted your view carefully, and if we decide to make you an offer, we will come back to you on that point. May we leave it at that for now?**

The remaining stages

This stage may repeat the information given during the introductory phase (Chapter 4, page 77), or you may add to whatever was said then. In either case, repetition is useful, as it is quite likely that the candidate has not picked up or remembered what was said during the opening remarks.

5. **We have more candidates to see this week, after which we will be inviting the shortlisted candidates back to meet the manufacturing director, the site manager and myself, probably during the last week of the month. Are there any dates that week when you would not be available?**

R1. *That will be fine. I am free all that week.*
R2. *I hope you will be able to make your decision fairly soon, as I have another offer in the pipeline.*
R3. *Unfortunately I'm abroad for two weeks starting on Saturday. I hope this won't prevent you considering me, as I'm very keen on the post.*

R1 is straightforward.

R2 may or may not be the truth. It may simply be an attempt to bring pressure to bear. The situation is similar to that discussed in Chapter 4, pages 80–82.

On the other hand, if you think this may be a highly suitable candidate, you may need to be more forthcoming, while still refusing to be pressurized:

S.   **Thank you for telling us. There is no reason why our decision should be delayed, and if we decide to shortlist you, I will certainly contact you within the next two days at most.**

R3 is a nuisance, but if it is likely that you will want the candidate, you must work around it. A week's delay is a small price to pay for the right person who may need to give several months' notice.

Leaving a good final impression

In concluding an interview, you should be aware of the fact that your candidates may turn up later as customers, working for your suppliers or competitors or even as interviewers on the other side of the table. They are certain to be part of your wider public, and are likely to know customers and other staff. If you do not employ them now, you may need them for a subsequent vacancy; possibly even for this one, if the first choice turns you down.

All this indicates that the farewells, however the interview has gone, must be courteous and friendly. You should show the candidate out of the room smilingly, ensure that all belongings have been gathered up, and that he or she is clear about what will happen next.

It is essential that you make no remarks that suggest how you view the candidate; even a cheery 'See you again, I hope' may be misinterpreted. Inexperienced interviewers may feel pressure to make some evaluative comment, but this must be sternly resisted.

7.   **Well, there we are, Mr Jones. Thank you very much for coming to see us. Did you have a coat?**

On the way out

Very tense candidates may only relax when they believe the end is in sight. Then, once in a while, if a reassuring, friendly presence is around, they may feel the sense of rapport you have striven for unsuccessfully throughout the interview, and open up with amazing frankness. This is an additional reason for one of the interviewers to conduct the candidate out personally.

8. Not too painful, I hope?

R1. *No, very fair. I enjoyed it.*

R2. *OK, but I wasn't sure I got on the right wavelength with the interviewer in the corner. I thought everyone else was friendly.*

R3. *It feels better now. To tell the truth, I was scared they were going to ask what happened at Grey's. Anyhow, it's all over now.*

R4. *I get so nervous at these things. My counsellor tells me that's perfectly normal, which is reassuring.*

Any attempt to follow up will need to be made exceedingly carefully, and may easily fail. However, walking slowly down the corridor, or in the lift, you may feel it is worth trying.

R2 might suggest a follow-up:

S.   **Oh, yes, Bill is quite a character. He can seem rather formidable at first meeting. Heart of gold, really. Did he stop you from doing your best?**

For R3, we might venture the gentle response:

S.   **Oh yes, I did wonder how things had been for you at Grey's, but I didn't like to ask. I guess they must have been pretty tough?**

For R4, something like this might have a chance of working:

S.   **Yes. I hate being interviewed myself; I think we all do. What other good advice does your counsellor give?**

If, in any of these cases, you find you are able to keep the conversation going, you may be inclined to do so as long as useful information seems forthcoming. However, you must be aware that other candidates may be waiting and there is a danger of giving information obtained in the post-interview euphoria undue weight.

Making an offer

You should resist the temptation to make a hasty decision. Even if the offer of employment is only made verbally, it can still be taken as a legally binding contract. Larger organizations often have recruitment and selection procedures that specify who is allowed to appoint and dismiss employees.

Usually the person who chairs the interview panel has the responsibility of bringing together the assessments of all the other interviewers so that a decision that all can live with can be made. If it is not possible to reach a consensus decision, the panel chair will have the responsibility of deciding what to do. If it is totally impossible to agree on which candidate to appoint, it may be better to appoint no one rather than someone whose suitability for the post is doubted by some of the interviewers.

You should be quite clear at the outset what your role is in the making of the decision. If you are a member of the panel, do your views inform someone else's decision, or will you be part of the decision? If you are the chair, will you make the decision alone, draw in the other members or have to consult someone not party to the interview? Early clarity can save later disagreement.

After all the interviews have been completed, you will need to review your notes against the person specification and, along with the other interviewers, assess the strengths of each candidate against the requirements of the job. This can be a time-consuming process and depending on the number of candidates seen and the time of day when the interviews have been completed, may be better done on the following day. It is, however, wise not to have a long gap between the interviews and making the assessment, as memory tends to distort over the passage of time.

Your notes will help you recall each candidate and overcome the errors discussed in Chapter 3. You will also find it helpful to use the matrix described in Chapter 2. This will help you consider each candidate systematically and to reduce the influence of any personal preferences. The matrix will also form a record, showing the basis for your eventual decisions. It is wise to record the reasons for deciding which candidate will be offered the job and why the other candidates are deemed not suitable for appointment.

There are times, however, when there is a need to make the decision while the candidates are still on the premises.

The advantages of doing this include:

- A good candidate, who may have other offers, can be secured before the chance is lost.
- If the candidate rejects the offer, it may be transferred to another while all are still available. But this needs to be handled very carefully, as otherwise the other candidate may feel that he or she is a poor second.
- The process can be speeded up.
- Any necessary bargaining can be done much faster, possibly more effectively, face to face.

The disadvantages include:

- All candidates must be held until the decision is made.
- There may be undue pressure to make a hasty decision.
- It may not be possible to carry out checks.

---

6. **Mr Jones, we have thought very carefully about all you have told us, and decided that, subject to references and a medical, we would like to offer you the post, at a salary of £25,000.**

R1. *Thank you very much. May I say now that I am delighted to accept and look forward to joining you.*

R2. *That's good news. Would you object if I think about it before giving you my answer?*

R3. *Thank you. I had hoped you could include a car. Do I take it that you are not able to offer me one?*

R4. *I've been thinking very carefully about our discussion while I was waiting, and I've decided the post is not what I am seeking. Thank you very much for the offer, but I prefer to step down.*

R1 calls for no comment.

R2 makes a very reasonable request. You may reply:

S. **Please do, but may we have your response soon? Could you manage to come back to us by tomorrow evening, please?**

R3 may be the start of bargaining which you cannot avoid. Your response will depend on how much you want the candidate, whether you believe there are others nearly as suitable, and how much flexibility your organization can give you.

R4 may prompt you to probe:

S. **Oh, I'm sorry to hear that. Would you like to tell us why?**

If you are very keen to employ the candidate, you will start to bargain, with the probe:

S. **That is very sad. The salary is tied to a large extent by what we pay to our existing staff, but we would be prepared to raise the offer to £26,000, if this would help.**

Depending on the outcome, you may inform the rejected candidates immediately, if they are still available, or later by phone or post when everything is final.

Providing feedback

Some organizations offer candidates the opportunity to receive feedback after the interview. Others do not, believing that this form of discussion may encourage unsuccessful and dissatisfied candidates to take out discrimination claims. Most claims are taken out by people who feel that they have been unfairly and badly treated. If candidates feel that they have gained something from the process, even if this was not an offer of employment, they are less likely to feel aggrieved. Provision of good-quality feedback can give candidates something positive to take away and use to improve their chances of success at subsequent interviews.

The purpose of giving feedback should be to help the candidate, not to give the provider any satisfaction. You should always remember that the candidate has the right to reject the feedback and ignore any suggestions you might make. You should, therefore, not attempt to force feedback on to candidates immediately after the interview. Rather it is better to say that feedback will be available should the candidate want it and then tell them who to contact. Leaving it up to them allows those whose pride has been hurt the chance of passing the opportunity by or at least giving them time to recover from their disappointment.

Good-quality feedback is based on the evidence gathered about the candidate and its assessment against the person specification. It should be given in a way that is designed to be helpful and will not overwhelm the candidate with a detailed analysis of every word spoken and gesture made.

Any examples should be used to make a more general point. But the feedback should be specific. Avoid generalized comments such as:

- [ ] **The way you described your experience at Browns was not very good.**

This does little to help the candidate work out how to do it better next time. More useful feedback would be:

- [ ] **You did not give us sufficient information about your experience at Browns, so we were unable to decide whether you had achieved those remarkable sales figures alone or as part of the larger sales team. In the absence of anything to the contrary and because you spoke so much about the strong team spirit in the company, we had to conclude that the team had achieved the result.**

This tells the candidate that interviewers are able to detect attempts to claim personal achievement from collective efforts.

Many candidates know for themselves where they fell down during the interview. Therefore the process of giving feedback can actually be aimed at helping candidates to articulate for themselves what they can do differently next time. For example:

- [ ] **You saw the person specification and job description we sent out before the interview. Do you have any ideas about where the major gaps were between your application and what we were looking for?**

Most candidates will have a good idea, as R1 below indicates, but others may need to be gently guided towards realizing why they were not appointed.

R1. *I guess my experience in conducting major sales campaigns was not as extensive as you were wanting. And I must admit that I did not present myself very well. I got myself muddled up. Nerves I guess.*

R2. *Not really. I thought that I had everything covered.*

S **What about your project management experience? We were looking for someone who had had considerable experience, as our projects are worth millions, involve nearly 100 people and last for about two years. We did not think that you are quite ready to handle that scale of operation. Perhaps in a couple more years. . .**

R3. *I am really disappointed. I was sure I was the best candidate.*

You should never get caught in the trap of comparing the appointed candidate's strengths with those of someone not appointed. Rather you can say, gently but firmly:

S **We felt that you still have some way to go. For example, we said that the ability to speak a foreign language was desirable. You might think about improving your French. We were also seeking excellent computer skills. While we know you are very good on spreadsheets, you might improve your use of databases.**

The ultimate aim of finishing off the interview process in this way is to leave the candidates feeling that they were given a fair chance to present themselves to the best of their ability and that they have learnt something helpful from the experience.

Induction and early training

Before closing your file on the interview, remember that the assessment is possibly one of the most thorough given to any employee. Therefore the exploration of the appointed candidate's skills, experience and knowledge will provide useful information about their immediate and subsequent development needs.

It is rare that the chosen candidate will be perfect in every aspect of the job. It is likely that during the interview, some weakness or gap in his or her skills or experience may have been identified.

Generally the induction period is seen solely as being the time during which the new appointee is helped to settle into the new place of work quickly. However, it can also be used to provide training to deal with these perceived gaps or weaknesses. You can use the interview assessment to feed into a personal development plan which can lay the ground for monitoring progress during the probationary period. It can also be used as the basis for the first appraisal meeting.

Bibliography

Chartered Institute of Personnel and Development (CIPD) (1991) *Interview Skills Training: Practice packs for trainers*, CIPD, London
Dale, M (1995) *Successful Recruitment and Selection*, Kogan Page, London
Dale, M (1996) *How to be a Better Interviewer*, Kogan Page, London
Edenborough, R (1996) *Effective Interviewing*, Kogan Page, London
Grayson, P (ed) (2000) *The Recruitment and Retention Handbook*, Gee Publishing, London
Hackett, P (1998) *The Selection Interview*, CIPD, London
Roberts, G (1997) *Recruitment and Selection: A competency approach*, CIPD, London
Shackleton, V (1989) *How to Pick People for Jobs*, Fontana, London
Smalley, L R (1999) *Interviewing and Selecting High Performers*, Kogan Page, London

From the interviewee's point of view

Corfield, R (1998) *How You Can Get That Job! Application forms and letters made easy*, Kogan Page, London
Corfield, R (1999) *Successful Interview Skills*, 2nd edn, Kogan Page, London
Greenwood, D (1995) *The Job-hunter's Handbook: An A-Z of tried and tested techniques*, Kogan Page, London
Parkinson, M (1994) *Interviews Made Easy: How to get the psychological advantage*, Kogan Page, London
Parkinson, M (2001) *The Times Graduate Job-hunting Guide*, Kogan Page, London
Yate, M J (2001) *Great Answers to Tough Interview Questions: How to get the job you want*, 5th edn, Kogan Page, London

Sources of
reference

ACAS, *Recruitment and Induction Advisory Booklet,* available from ACAS Publications, PO Box 16, Earl Shilton, Leicester LE9 877

Chartered Institute of Personnel and Development is the professional body. CIPD House, Camp Road, Wimbledon, London SW19 4UX; tel: 020 8971 9000; Web site: www.ipd.co.uk

Commission for Race Equality, Elliot House, 10–12 Allington Street, London SW1E 5EH; tel: 020 7828 7022

Disabilities Rights Commission, Freepost MID 02614, Stratford-upon-Avon CV37 9BR; tel: 08457 622633; Web site: www.drc-gb.org

Employers Forum for Disabilities, Nutmeg House, 70 Gainsford Street, London SE1 2NY; tel: 020 7403 3020; Web site: www.employers-forum.co.uk

Equal Opportunities Commission, Overseas House, Quay Street, Manchester M3 3HN; tel: 0161 833 9244

Recruitment and Employment Confederation represents employment agencies. 36–38 Mortimer Street, London W1N 7RB; tel: 020 7323 4300; Web site: www.fres.co.uk

Chambers of Commerce, Business Links and the various employers associations may also be able to provide advice.

Increasingly, Web sites are available. Some are publicly accessible but others are available only to subscribers. Many are American and even though they appear to use the same words and concepts, you need to check that you are in a Web site coming from the right country as legal systems vary.

Index